A Poetic Pilgrimage

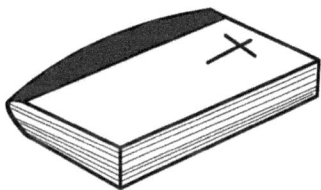

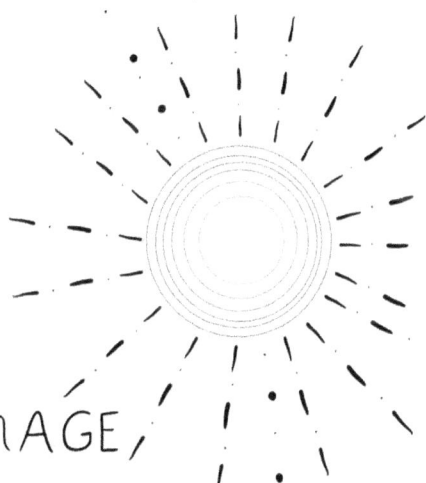

A POETIC PILGRIMAGE

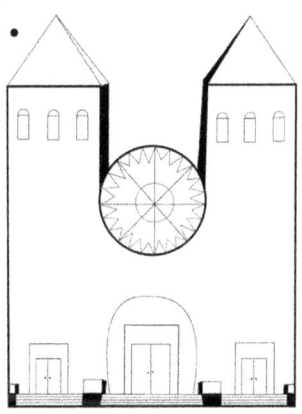

Olivia Knepp

♡

A compilation of poems portraying the intricate journey
from youthful naivety to seasoned wisdom♡

Contents

Contents

In the World

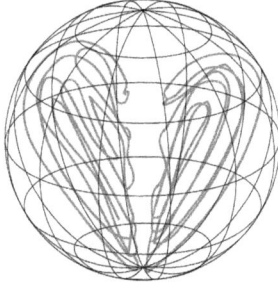

Contents

Isolation Season I

Contents

Isolation Season II

Contents

Isolation Season III

Contents

In His Hands I

Contents

In His Hands II

Contents

In His Hands III

This book is dedicated to all the beautiful souls that make up God's creation. I hope and pray it speaks to you, inspires you, and provides hope regardless of what you have gone through or continue to endure. The verses found throughout the book were chosen to coordinate with certain poems, and they will be found on the page following each poem it relates to. The World English Bible (WEB) was selected for the bible verses because of its smooth comprehension, but I encourage you to delve deeper and compare translations as you read. Personally, I favor the New King James Version (NKJV) for my devotional time, yet I recognize everyone's reading preference varies. If a verse resonates with you, I urge you to explore the entire chapter for further context and insight. I have organized my writings primarily by the date they were written, not only to illustrate the journey they encapsulate, but to show that walking with God, both mentally and physically, is not a clear-cut path.

Our stories may differ, but one truth remains: the human condition involves moments of struggle and triumph, with each day and every season igniting varying emotions. This book serves as tangible evidence that trials, through patience and perseverance, yields wisdom and fruitful blessings. As James 1:3 reveals, *the testing of our faith produces perseverance,* a refining process essential for spiritual growth. Just as gold is purified through fire, our faith is strengthened through challenges, leading to a mature and complete faith. Whether dealing with navigating choices, the complexity of relationships, battles of mental health, situations of loss, or the feelings of being down on our luck- *change is constant.*

When facing difficulties, we may question the purpose of our trials, but James 1 reminds us that these impactful moments are the ingredients to the development of perseverance, while Hebrews 11 further informs us that faith assures God's promises, even when we cannot see them. Then you have Psalm, which provides a template of mindfulness and a gameplan for action for each day, no matter what that day may bring. Each book of the bible has wisdom to provide, experiences we can relate to, and truths to be shared. To apply these truths, we must embrace trials as growth opportunities, strengthen our faith by immersing ourselves in God's promises, and support one another through challenges. Amidst any circumstances, goodness can be found, and further goodness awaits. *Faith is confidence in hope and the assurance of what we cannot see yet.*

This isn't a book based around conversion, but a book cultivated with the mission to provide hope.

We are all made in the image of God. We are not perfect, but we are uniquely beautifully valued in God's eyes. Our hills and valleys are here to provide testimony, inspiration, direction, and hope to ourselves and others.

This is a gentle reminder that you are loved, you are never alone, and your experiences are never in vain. Let this book be a reminder that our faith, tested and refined, is a testament to the strength of our hope. May we face trials with joy, rooted in the assurance of God's promises, and let our lives reflect His glory. Amen.

Acknowledgements

I want to give a gratitude-filled shoutout to my friends and loved ones who have stuck by my side and remained true in every season of my life thus far. A memorious thank you to those who sat with me at all hours of the day, and who walked alongside me during my poetic pilgrimage, both during the writing process and outside of the writing process.

A special thank you to my dear friend Avery-for not only listening to my work and your unceasing moral support, but also for providing a second set of eyes through the final editing process. I know the recent months have been busy for you, and I am so grateful for your time and heart.

Thank you to my life-long friend Laura for always being a sister I can count on. Your constant encouragement and support are more appreciated than you know. Even when we are 500 miles from each other, I know you are but a guaranteed phone call away.

Thank you to my brother Ethan; our relationship runs thicker than blood, and I am so proud and grateful to call you my sibling.

Most importantly, I want to grant a never-ending thank you to the Creator for giving me the inspiration, the strength, the direction, the wisdom, and the discernment to transform my emotions into writing. What started as a form of therapy, turned into a Spirit-led passion project that has been more healing and rewarding than I can physically describe. I couldn't have done it without the love of the Father, the encouragement of Jesus Christ, and the gifts of the Spirit.

I am forever grateful to everyone who listened to me speak as God revealed the words that captivated the story I wish share, even if they only thought my poetry was no more than a form of expression and a hobby. Your kind words and encouragement, along with God's guiding direction inspired me to share my story with the world, regardless of who, or how many hear it. I pray that my words provide peace, strength, hope, and make those who need it feel a little less alone.

Let the pilgrimage begin.

I

IN THE WORLD

I

Sea Sickness

I feel like I am lost at sea.

Drifting away,
no one is looking for me.

My heart is a treasure,
but it has been forgotten.

Used and abused-
my love is rotting.

I feel like I am drowning,
drowning to the bottom of the sea,

sunken to the bottom-
my feelings and me.

I feel like I am drowning,

and no one is looking for me,

and when they do-
they just leave me be.

Because this treasure has rotted.

This treasure is forgotten-
used and abused,

painfully discarded,
painfully forgotten.

Now I am sitting here,
the situation remains crystalline clear.

The beauty within me locked away-
out of instinctual protection towards what remains.

I am just a castaway,
caught in a riptide.

My heart has been shattered,
my spirit has died.

Running from love-
what will I find?

My heart has been shattered-
left behind.

Will anyone come rescue me?

LDR

Lana sings,
I cry.

Six years,
and I sigh.

Turmoil for twelve-

*but who's counting,
right?*

Racing Thoughts

Give me a reason to stay-
        give me a reason to stay.

I watch the words pour out like a leaking faucet,
        observing closely to how my thoughts subtly maneuver my lips.

        Does it look right?
        How does it sound?

        Is it too much-

        an ultimatum,
        or common ground?

        Am I too vague?

        Do you assume my hope in a correct response?

This is not a test.
        There is no wrong.

What I am truly asking is-
        if there a reason for my heart to stay?

My heart yearns home,
        and home is with you.

        Do you see a home within my heart too?

K.

why do I hurt?
This is not easy.

XXX

Sometimes I feel caught in a game.

I am aware of who I am,
but I cannot determine if your point of view is refrained.

You tell me the good-
like my beauty.

The bad-
how you do not want me.

And the ugly-
our history.

Like heroin,
what makes me so high,

can bring me so low.

You are keeping Xs on your exs,

counting marks like you are counting cards-
baby don't you know that can get you in trouble?

Unfair Advantage

I am dealt into this game.

The cards I play,
        I am already holding.

1 Corinthians 13:4-7

Love is patient and is kind.
Love doesn't envy.

Love doesn't brag, is not proud,

5 doesn't behave itself inappropriately,
doesn't seek its own way,

is not provoked,
takes no account of evil;

6 doesn't rejoice in unrighteousness,
but rejoices with the truth;

7 bears all things, believes all things,
hopes all things, and endures all things.

Hangman

In a game of hangman-
     I am left guessing.

I have put myself on ban,
     but that only leads to your professing.

I have played this game many times.

     I ultimately have complied my own set of strategies-
     yet I have learned these are crimes.

     I cannot manipulate,
     nor create fallacies.

Trying to follow by the book,
     but we are succumbed to the mortal senses,

     we are mistaken-

     negotiating,
     associating,

     convincing pretenses.

It all is fun and games until someone gets hurt.

     When I am in your scope,
     I am hung for observation.

It sometimes seems okay when you flirt,

     yet one false move leaves me begging for your salvation.

     Some acts are just never forgiven-
     my forgiveness is a given.

Counting xs like you are counting cards-

     one head,
     four extremities,
     one torso,

     frequently with little regard,
     a mark is laid on me.

     I keep telling myself it could be worse, so.

Self-Centered or Broken?

Inside I remain broken.
       I have a love that remains hidden.

Even if I wanted it to flow,
       my feelings are selectively open.

Uniquely me-
       they say they love,

       come as you are-
       until they rip me apart.

What a wonderful heart made of gold,
       until they do not favor the responses they are told-

       the promises unkept,
       the secrets hidden,

       the broken hearts,
       and the indecisiveness even.

Then there is the storm that rages within me.

       The outpour of words that tell me everything I can and cannot be-

       I can or cannot have.

My heart breaks,

       my energy drains-
       no insurance to cover the emotional damage that the storm has claimed.

Just another pretty face,
       do as they say.

My heart aches for something secure-
       something more.

       Am I selfish to feel this way?

The Sun

The sun feels welcoming,
        but your smile is warmer.

Tormented by day,
        I may sleep soundly at night,

        but I wake to find the dreams that kept me in slumber were but only dreams.

I tell myself I am cleansing,
        I am healing-

        do I know where I am going?

Is it too much for you to ask me to stay?

        It is selfish of me to seek validation this way.

Do you think I wanted to go?
        Do you think I wanted to leave you behind?

        I could never do so since you are always on my mind.

So I wait,

        and I sit,
        and I think to myself-

        how there is no one like you,
        there is no one else.

But I cannot expect you to proclaim my homecoming,

        and I cannot expect you to want me to stay.

        my battles remain my own battles,
        yet I lay awake thinking of you-

        no distance can truly keep me away.

In my heart it reigns true-

        my constant introspection about you.

I ran away from home,
        please come to my rescue.

Psalm 34:18

Yahweh is near to those
who have a broken heart,

and saves those who are crushed in spirit.

Honeydew

Thank you sweet dear for opening your home up-
every laugh shared with you felt like sunshine.

But 40 days without rain in combination
with the barreling velocity that came my way,

resulted in tumultuous dust storms,
which began to suffocate me-

I had to bear goodbye.

How Long?

How long will it last?

I pray forever-
I pray by the grace of God that these trials are over.

Let My Garden Grow

Is this where peace is found-
in an environment with constant storms raging all around?

I ask myself,
'When will it end?'

You see-

I remember the days of sunshine,
prior to the tormenting pain,

chilling winds,
and raging storms.

I know rain brings growth-
without the rain we would not grow.

I remind myself the storm is necessary-
everything has been.

Even the days I am drowning from the outpour,
I still persevere today.

I do not know when the storm will end,
for that is beyond my control.

I can find peace knowing it is all part of His perfect plan.

Let the waters flow,

and my garden grow-
tall.

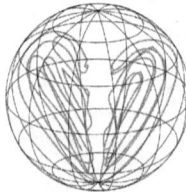

Galatians 6:7-9

Do not be deceived.
God is not mocked,

for whatever a man sows,
that he will also reap.

8 For he who sows to his own flesh will
from the flesh reap corruption.

But he who sows to the Spirit
will from the Spirit reap eternal life.

9 Let's not be weary in doing good,

for we will reap in due season,
if we don't give up.

Broken Home

My dreams are flooded with other women and rivalries-
I contemplate God's message as I lay on your sheets.

I innately look away as you fidget on your phone-

could it be to protect my heart from what I do not want to be shown,

or an instinctual response,
refraining my thoughts from catalyzing into words made known?

I breathe heavy as the base rocks my body-
you'd think by now I would be desensitized to the electromagnetic energy.

I cried myself to sleep as Lana sung me melodramatic lullabies,
with the embedded words of flattery from the night rattling in my mind,

but I grew homesick-
and I can trust you will always come back around.

No timestamp of certainty,
just the innate knowing you will always crave me.

Sweet desires and innocent smiles are shattered like looking in a cracked mirror,
by the force of clouded judgement and hurtful conjectures.

It is like you say things out of blind intent to hurt me.

An educated guess in a game of battleship,
that only brings down the vessel that is my heart.

It is moments like this I ponder on the idea of settling,
or swearing myself to a life of celibacy.

Your words unknowingly constrict me,

gripping me beyond erotic asphyxiation,
tighter than plastic around my physical body-

but the look in your eye tells me differently.

My heart tries to tell you to stop,

but your words were like a hot iron disabling me-
branding a scar on the walls of my mind long past physical recovery.

Maybe if I do as you want you will look at me differently?

In a world quick to honor me an unqualified maternal award,
it is your opinion I carry with me wherever I go.

I am not your sex doll,
'Do you realize how your words impair me?'

Self-mediated Therapy

Creating a body no one can have,
        because my heart is still with *him*-

        and I would be dead before I let another afflict upon me the way *they* once did.

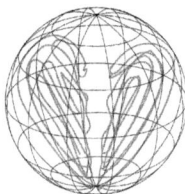

II

ISOLATION SEASON

II

The Haunting

By circumstance or chance-
I find myself alone again.

Once surrounded by faces I am now haunted by their memory-
my life could have gone so differently.

The only face I see is my own reflection staring back at me.

The ghosts of my past once haunted my room-
now their essence is attached to the objects I hold onto.

An orphaned owl,
the commissioned one of one that hangs on my wall,

picture frames wiped clean of any momentous occupancy-
are all now but an echoing reminder of what once was.

Even when empty-
the once was still haunts me.

Every season offered the chance to start anew,

but I would pick,
and I would chase-

I did not listen,
and I did not learn.

My attempts to run left me exhausted and burned.
I was depleted after the contents of my insides had been ripped open-

now I am reaping the attempted vision.

The effort of my causes,
left bare and alone-

I only wish to start anew.

If only I could bring with me the souls that once haunted my room.

Mother Knows Best

My mother told me not to play with fire.
  The costs were visible.

  Numb fingers and singed hair,
  the destructive nature was apparently clear.

My mother told me not to play with strangers,
  and I was very much aware.

  Not everyone is who they portray upon observation,
  and the right intentions are not always there.

My mother warned me not to dance with the devil,
  but the wager was not transparent.

  I could not fathom the destruction it would bear-

  the devil whispering in woman's ear,
  knowing shed latch onto the deceit he shared.

He has played these cards in crime.

  She was unaware she already lost,

  until she is forced to fold-
  for the last time.

My mother warned me of all these things-

  their destructive nature,
  and what it would bring.

  She forewarned the devil is a cheat who will take my everything,
  and I still played the devil in a round of life.

  Cheated out of my heart, my sanity-
  I willingly handed over everything in my strife.

But Adam and Eve chose this game of life,

  and because of my own actions-
  I am paying the price.

Genesis 3:2-5

The woman said to the serpent,

"We may eat fruit from the trees
of the garden,

3 but not the fruit of the tree
which is in the middle of the garden.

God has said, 'You shall not eat of it.
You shall not touch it, lest you die.'"

4 The serpent said to the woman,
"You won't really die,

5 for God knows that in the day you eat it,
your eyes will be opened,

and you will be like God, knowing good and evil."

Seasons Changing

Every day I am reminded of you.

The early rise,
so young and full of hope-

the warmth it brings with its morning glow.

I am enveloped with warmth,
resembling the comfort you would bring,

as it sits high beaming down on me.

The cold-blooded world is awakened into motion,

in movement as we used to be-

working together in gracious harmony.

The sun slowly falls,
reminding me of a departing beauty I cannot control-

a fiery blaze that still captivates my soul.

I can only watch with my eyes-
what brought me great warmth dwindles from my right side.

I can try to chase you,
with all my power I run,

so that I am always in proximity to the setting sun.

But I will never catch up,

before I know it-
you are gone.

The warmth becomes no more than a memory-
a memory of the time I was in love.

Left out in the cold,

the goodness in my life appears-
gone.

Ecclesiastes 3:1

For everything there is a season,

and a time for every purpose under heaven.

Master Copy

'Can you play that song one more time?

> Pause this scene-
> hit rewind?'

If you do not know,

> the remote broke long ago-
> no control.

The VCR tossed onto the road-

> the home movies trashed,
> any remaining,
>
> bear no home.
>
> Taped over...
> 'with something better.'
>
> Soiled.

The copies have turned to soot in the last fire.

> That she had lit here-
> that you let in.

All the memories-

> all the good,
> and the bad,
>
> sit in a trash bin.

Amongst the rubble,
> the few left ruminating having been used up,
>
> to record your new smash demo-
> or should I say babel.

Who am I to judge,
> and who am I to point the blame?
>
> Who am I to call out the culprit(s)-
>
> for trashing the VCR and all my favorite tapes?

I still have the master copies,
> if you ever wish to see,
>
> or listen to my most treasured moments,
> of you and me.

The Last Letter (I)

You burn every letter I write-
    actively dismissing the words that burn within my heart.

I promise these are the last words I am addressing to you.

My words are short and sweet and may make you inclined to read-
    but only God knows what you will truly do.

Part of me has my doubts-
    deep down I know I have won.

I always opened myself up to receive what you let in.

        Like a passive draft,
        I let myself be chilled in the hopes to see you crack a grin-

        the cost of your priceless smile makes me dismiss the pain I feel within.

I justify the chill because I am aware you are broken,

        and there is no guarantee with an *'As Is' product-*
        that is a given.

Regardless of our connection and the coeval circumstances-
    I am not your token.

        'Have you forgotten,
        I am only human?'

Made of the same earth as you with a gently crafted soul.

        Living in a world of illusion-
        or maybe chess is a more fitting description.

You say, *'I am strong'-*
    are you waiting for me to crack then?

        Do you anticipate me to show weakness,
        or to prove your conjectures wrong?

        Is it too selfish for me to dream of hearing one last sweet song?

I read between the lines-
    or the lies.

        I justify every rhyme and note out of tune.

I remember what once was,
    or what could have been.

        I wait for the song to go back into a familiar swoon.

The Last Letter (II)

No longer can I overlook the destruction you cause.

> You have set fire to a one of one,
> shattering what was labeled *'Handle With Care.'*

> *There is very little concern to the precious art,*
> *and sometimes I think you are aware.*

Like precious porcelain,
> the fixed cracks are mended with gold.

> *I will let you walk away without paying what is owed.*

> Never are you held liable,
> I let you get away again and again with the same crime.

> *For Christ has paid for it-*

> *in reality,*
> *you do not owe me a dime.*

Who am I to hold a grudge?

> Yet I have always let you come back for more,

> handing you a pass to cause havoc in my life-
> destroying aspects that I worked so hard for.

I have always thought things would be different,
> but that is where I am wrong.

> *Cycles repeat like clockwork,*
> *and only God knows if I will ever hear that familiar song.*

Some would think it is deja vu.
> *I try to see the world through God's eyes too.*

> But my attempts do not justify the sin-
> because I am human,

> therefore,
> I do not fit the job description.

> *It is not my job to fix what is broken,*

> even when the pottery is marked *'As Is.'*

> *I am not The Potter.*

You try to burn what is rightfully mine-
> arson is yet another crime.

The unnecessary hurt caused-

> the mind games,
> the debates,
> the lies.

> This is not a game for anyone to play,
> *especially with Christ on one's side.*

I politely step away-

> and without two,
> there is not much of a game to play.

You are left alone-

> *bullying ricochets into torment within your own soul.*

> *I have tried to show you the right way,*
> *but I will not be a pawn in a game with the devil today.*

Out of love I am walking away-

> *through the strength of the One who made me,*
> *I am learning to be okay.*

Psalm 71:20

You, who have shown us many
and bitter troubles,

you will let me live.

You will bring us up again
from the depths of the earth.

Wasted Vessel

Wasted Vessel,

> misused potential-
> forgotten purpose,

> your body has become a raging furnace.

Burning and charring anything that goes in,
> or that becomes proximally too close.

I have formulated excuse after excuse for the constant misuse.

> In reality,
> it is abuse,

> *resulting from the life you continually chose.*

A perfectly imperfect world so often molded by delusion.

> The effects imprinting infractions-
> emotions catalyzed by confusion.

> *I recognize the fired attempts to spark a reaction.*

Choices acted on through the enemy's deception-

> has anyone taught you not to play with fire,
> or how to protect your heart from wrongful desire?

> *I have grown aware of both your intentions and my heart's desire.*

So often-
> you aim to capture others into the net that has overtaken your life.

> *You made it verbally clear,*

> *you like it here-*
> *within the walls of your mental prison.*

> And as much love as I have for you,
> I cannot condone being dragged within.

I was once entangled-

> yet God made a way by cutting a hole,
> and let me swim away free.

He promises the more I tread these open waters,
> *the stronger I will be.*

> *I explore the holy waters within the sea of opportunity.*

Countless times I have tried to bring you out here with me,
> *but you believe the net's comfort is the safest place to be.*

This world was never supposed to be what is most true.

The only one to blame for your downfall is you-
and I will not let myself drown,

awareness is my instinctual cue.

I engage with awareness,
but it is not to satisfy your mere beck and call.

I see the traps laid marked out with your own downfall.

Like an alligator stalking its prey,
you wait for the best chance to devour someone's all.

I am letting God remove myself from this ensnaring trawl-
the mess that you have gotten yourself into.

I will always mourn the loss of the wasted vessel that is you.

Isaiah 43:18-19

Don't remember the former things,
and don't consider the things of old.

19 Behold, I will do a new thing.

It springs out now.
Don't you know it?

I will even make a way in the wilderness,
and rivers in the desert.

...NO.

No was never really in my vocabulary-
　　　maybe I never had the chance to say it enough.

My worth at times appeared voluntary-
　　　a persistent inconsistency imprinted the feeling of a 'lack of.'

　　　My feelings swept under a rug.

I tried so hard to cling to what I knew.

　　　The good in my life-
　　　I held a firm grasp to.

Who am I to make such a conjecture?

　　　To deem what is good versus what is better,

　　　and what is best-
　　　I never knew,

　　　due to my clouded judgement that I held onto.

The poison I ingested,
　　　the thorns in my side,

　　　it was all I ever knew so it must be best-
　　　right?

For the poison brought an intoxicating feeling,
　　　one that leaves you clinging to a world of delusion-

　　　and in certain seasons roses would bloom.

　　　My eyes encapsulated and my body overtaken,
　　　by their sweet-smelling perfume.

　　　The pain seemed worth it too.

The pain would remain despite the highs,

　　　the numbness would wear away,
　　　and the roses heads would decay,

　　　be cut off,

　　　and tossed away to die-
　　　leaving me high and dry.

The good never seemed to last and the pain would remain,

　　　the desire to love and be loved,
　　　was more soul crushing than cocaine.

It took me 23 years to realize the problem is not the person or my desire for the high-

the problem was where I was looking-
and where people so often lean into.

The good is temporal,
but the pain is too.

There is only one everlasting remedy to the hills and valleys of life.

The answer is Jesus,
that is who I cling to.

Humans are imperfect,
but He is the only friend I need to continually run to.

Dreamer

You are always in my dreams.

False hope,
or potential possibility?

All that could have or have not been.

I hold onto these dreams like memories,

I would never release them to the wind.

But prayers come true-
sometimes hopes and dreams do too.

So do not laugh at me for holding onto mine.

Some call it a false sense of hope,
I call it divine time.

Call me a dreamer,
I know that which is mine.

Job 33:14-15

"For God speaks once,

yes twice,
though man pays no attention.

15 In a dream,
in a vision of the night,

when deep sleep falls on men,
in slumbering on the bed."

Willa Mae, Willa Mae

Why is it the ones I desire so close,
　　　are the ones who slowly drift the furthest from me?

Willa Mae, Willa Mae-
　　　a name filled with sweet memories.

Flashbacks in the timeline are compiled with-

　　　consignment thrift finds,

　　　genuine belly laughter,

　　　and coffee trademarked by pungent potency.

Willa Mae, Willa Mae-
　　　how our times together have expired from me.

　　　Friends that once frolicked in child-like wonder and sweet harmony-
　　　they once seemed to always be right beside me.

My memories attributed by a seven-year period,
　　　that consistently left me melancholy.

　　　When one said *'Farewell,'*
　　　another said *'Hello.'*

　　　An empty void that lost occupancy,

　　　once again filled and contracting a new role-
　　　metamorphosis.

Willa Mae, Willa Mae-
　　　a name I held so dear.

　　　We were the best of friends,
　　　we were the worst of friends-

　　　some would call it a setback.

　　　A half to a pair and without the other-
　　　it was defined as *lack.*

　　　Evidently attached-
　　　what has become of this?

Willa Mae, Willa Mae-
  can we give it one more try?

Please do not take my gentle heart and toss it aside.
  Forget about my life?

  They erased all the moments I was there-
  why?

Oh, how they made me cry.
  I burdened the apologies and I now realize that was not all right.

Willa Mae, Willa Mae-
  I let out another sigh,

  followed by tears of anger,

  hurt,
  remorse,
  and despise.

I put my trust into the Willa Maes in my life.

  They often relied on me to tend and mend to their own strife-
  I clung desperately onto what I thought was right.

  I never wanted to lose the goodness-
  despite the various types of smite.

Their words left me bruised and battered.

  Their actions left me alone in the cold-
  went astray.

The chaos they brought resulted in me fighting for my life.

  The mess they made,
  and I had to clean up and endure,

  only made my self-sufficiency more assure.

I am still here to tell the tale.

  Fool me once,

  twice,
  a third time-

  they will never.

  For that reason-
  I cannot condone another Willa Mae.

Occupancy has been filled-
  I send peace but, I also equally bear good riddance to her...them.

43

Present (I)

Present, Noun: the current moment or period of time.

You are told *'to remain present,'*
remain present to what is presently presented.

Remain within the beat-

in rhythm and in tune to a performance you have never rehearsed.

The recital co-occurring simultaneously to your first practice ever on earth.

The tempo appears comprised to *The Ticking Clock,*
in synchronization to the activity of *The Altering Sky.*

You watch the other dancers make the production look so simplistic,
you are unaware that your scope of view is unrealistic.

Others seemingly gracious movements pass you by,

through your limited frame of reference-
not a beat faster, nor a beat behind.

You prepare and plan for your next step in this dance entitled *'Life.'*

With so many models you hope to appear alike-
you just want to fit in.

Sometimes you mimic others' footsteps like copying test answers-

other times looking for words of advice and encouragement,
from the other dancers.

Both feel like a stab in your heart-
'was that a hot knife?'

The movements you observe and try upon suggestion-
are just not right.

The form and fluctuations are not intended for your body,
it is evident on stage that they do not come naturally.

After all *this is your assigned role in the dance of 'Life-'*
copying another's footsteps is just not right.

The other dancers' parts are uniquely appointed.

This reality check leaves you disappointed-
internally conflicted.

In self-reflection you ask yourself,
      'What *is* my role in this performance presently insisting and depicting?'

      It seems so easy to join in company,
      until you become off-rhythm from an uncalibrated movement.

      Feeling distant in apogee-
      a result of an unprepared shift in melody.

A desirous motive to fit right in,
      and do so graciously.

      You try arduously to plan your footing,

      but self-preservation causes delay with the visually surrounding motion-
      one false step leads to commotion.

Sometimes you are not to blame.

      Like a game of battleship,
      you do not know which dancer(s) intend to throw a swing or a hit,

      while rarely offering you a prelude tip-

      that is,
      their *true* intentions.

      Few genuinely understand the emotions behind their selfish actions.

      Regardless the unexpected sabotage leads you to trip-
      sometimes with the direct intent to make you fall.

It is unfathomable to you-

      but now your mind and footing are presently further off,
      causing you to collide into others oncoming trajectory.

      Who knew this dance could really turn into a brawl?

Present (II)

Present, Adjective: relating to now, for the time being; current.

> *I cannot tell what moves faster-*
> *my thoughts or the current change that co-occurs.*

Comorbidities coexisting,

often resisting-
designated sparring partners.

Consistency persisting,
often second-guessing.

When did the dance of 'Life' turn into a fight of finishing?
When is the final curtain call?

The continuous and incessant routines bounce and ricochet like particles,
contained within the bounds of the world's walls.

Instantaneous and uncontrolled,

colliding,
catalyzing,
changing trajectory-

sometimes terrorizing.

The environment itself is enough to leave you frozen (on stage)-
if not knocked out cold.

Present (III)

Present, Adjective: located in the immediate vicinity.

Inhale.

Contained by the walls of *'The Universal Theatre,'*
your preformed movements are no more than improv.

You now realize what you perceived as effortless graciousness-
is no more than the whole world firing movements like a kalashnikov.

You cannot blame yourself for the lack of preparation.

The truth is the world is ad-lib in motion.

Present (IV)

Present, Verb: to give (a gift or presentation) to someone; to bestow.

> *There is only One who is aware of every movement,*
> *of every outcome of every thought and entanglement-*

> *Who is even aware of every future development.*

Presenting prayers with a professing heart,
a doorway is open to a place of peace-

> *a break off stage,*
> *accompanied along with a fresh start.*

This place provides restoration-
a place capable of absorbing and annihilating the constant commotion.

You are still.

> When you are ready to step back out on stage,
> you become aware of a spotlight-

> you stop looking towards the company of *'The Universal Theatre,'*

> *With a fully-fledged heart,*
> *you look to the light to engage.*

> Shining bright this light begins guiding you intentionally,
> speaking to your heart the proper positional moves to *'Life,'*

> *without deception.*

Truth.

> Suddenly what seemed so hard to keep within timing and tune,
> no longer feels like a fight of exhaustion and doom.

> *The routine unfolds more beautifully than beyond comprehension.*

> You no longer second guess your motion,
> which allow you to start embracing your movements with great emotion.

> Sometimes you even begin to estimate the guiding light's next direction-

> at some points with great accuracy,
> and other times what comes next may leave you feeling perplexed.

But the spotlight never ceases.

> As your trust grows in the spotlight you do not grow weary-

> *only protected.*

When we accept God,
>He guides us in real time to the routine He has uniquely created.

>He makes room for every dancer's movement,
>the talents He has anointed-

>*with purpose-filled intention.*

Every partnered entanglement,
>the complex and unfathomable enchantment.

>*His routine is without malicious infringement.*

>He makes room because of *His love,*

>*grace,*
>*mercy,*
>*purpose,*

>*and peace.*

Without ceasing His love endures-
>*all because of the presently empty tomb.*

Isaiah 41:10

"Don't be afraid,
for I am with you.

Don't be dismayed,
for I am your God.

I will strengthen you.

Yes, I will help you.

Yes, I will uphold you
with the right hand of my righteousness."

Peace or in Pieces?

The waters are still-

    I tread with strength,
    because I have found restoration.

Once fighting uphill-

    I began questioning the distances' great lengths,

    of my own fabricated decisions.

My human nature once hoped to foresee the end-
    my heart and soul refused to bend.

    Refusing to release to the wind-
    the story I clung desperately onto.

    The only reality I knew.

As time went on,
    I denied admittance to the temporal energy's expend.

    I withdrew from the emergency fund,
    as an effort to provide a way for the story to mend.

    A wasteful attempt to buy more time to reiterate,

    to retaliate-
    to cling onto the lies I was fed.

    My stubborn psyche,
    pushing to see the finish line marked with a happy ending-

    the closing of the script I continued writing in my head.

Human nature-
    creatures of habit.

    I now realize my wrongful investments led to a loss of profit.

    My repetition of words and actions were never the right solution-
    they only resulted in loss of time and energy to the power of delusion.

The power was exhausted,
    leaving me feeling like a dunce.

    If I tried it once *(stubborn me)*,
    and then again (*fabricated reality)*,

    how can I expect a third attempt would exist as the desired cure-
    that my lone attempts would fix everything at once?

Risk-filled investments resulted in the repossession of my municipality's walls.

My losses left my temple unprotected,
my light exhausted,

and valuable pieces and jewels left unguarded.

Like a blacked-out city open for the ransacking and the taking,

the poisoning-
the tainting.

Without the guarding power to oversee the delicate light within me,
thieves came in and out to take,

what they could now openly reach and see.

Playing my heartstrings like a fiddle,

or bluntly breaking down my door-
they would even sometimes conspire their return for more.

With easy access they plotted against what remained.

Conspiring what they could sneakily take and then leave-
no concern for how their actions snowballed into further demolition and grief.

Leaving me in disbelief-
'How could someone I keep so close be a thief?'

It was the jewels they envied.

Desirous sin whispering into man's ear-
human nature.

Look at Adam and Eve,
examine Cane and Abel,

Joseph and his brothers,
Ahab and his wife,

Esau and Jacob.

They robbed my peace in a plot for the precious pieces.
The gems and jewels of my spirit-

my innocence,
my happiness,
and my peace.

Yet God has restored my worth through the purpose of the isolation season-
a restoration within a heart once filled with grief.

A newfound spirit overflowing with comfort and peace.

Hearts of Jealousy

The conniving smiles,
        green hearts of envy.

Whatever direction I move,

        like a shadow,
        they were close behind me.

Lack of self-awareness,
        a need for contemplation-

        it is said the herd blindly follows,
        but there is no guarantee they will listen.

Jealousy.

        Eyes watching me-
        stalking me.

        Glued to 'the reality TV.'

Like watching reruns of-

        'Gossip Girl,'

        their whole world,
        lacking direction,

        copying and pasting,

        my heart's ambition and decision-
        calling it their own.

Plagiarism.

        It is hypocritical,
        to both bash and follow,

        my life,
        my purpose-

        my *mission.*

        Discover your own ambition as He has written.

        My story is already taken.

Insomnia

Exhausted Body-
>   *restive or resistive?*

>   My beauty sleep is calling me by name,
>   but you occupy my head instead.

I write to keep busy-
>   you would tell me,

>   *'If that is what you believe.'*

9 P.M. moves to 2 A.M.

>   I pray to God that you leave,
>   *get out of my head...*

>   *even if a small part of me misses your bed.*

It is not the shared mattress I miss that keeps me up at night,

>   nor the house occasionally occupied by other girls,
>   invited in by your wandering eyes,

>   and not even the idea of sleeping alone makes me blue...
>   *it is really the home I miss that I once found inside of you.*

That was lost long ago,
>   and the locks had been changed.

>   *I could not get back in how I once did,*
>   *even before I started sleeping alone again.*

Like looking through a window of a place I once knew-

>   the furniture is different,
>   and what remains is rearranged.

>   Everything has changed into an *unsettling anew.*

Even if I was invited through the door the home is unrecognizable-
>   *it has morphed into a place that has become undesirable.*

I used to play pretend that I am okay with what you have done with the place-
>   *but those days are officially through.*

>   It has been years since I felt like I was lying next to the man I once knew.

>   *Finally in evident view-*
>   *a transpiration into an unwelcoming taboo.*

It is time for the charade to end and for the mask to be removed.
>   *I am alone again, but it is truly nothing new.*

My Pain, Your Muse.

Hallow and cold,
  empathy has no occupancy.

You make pleasure out of someone else's pain-
  self-serving gain.

  My own emotional downfall is your muse.

Only every offering the option to choose,
  when the choices presented would leave me deprecating.

  Completely depleting,
  anxiously stressing-

  left second-guessing.

I cannot win and now-

  I cannot look back.

  A lesson learned from the downfall of Lot's wife-
  for there is ultimate self-harm and loss in that act.

The was,

  the could have,

  the should have,

  the never been,

  the never known,

  every destruction along the way,
  has further carried me to this point on the road.

Those once so dear to me,
  I love you.

But no amount of love is enough to allow myself to destroy my temple for you.

So,
  I keep moving-
  forward.

57

The Next

Time feels frozen during adolescence but that is far from the truth-

> when proximal vision is filtered through the rose-colored glasses of youth.

The clock paces ever so slowly as life appears to be standing still.

> Change sweeps over in the form of overlooked seasons,
> you are always daydreaming of *the next* for some reason.

It appears like time is never moving fast enough-
> impatiently you wait for *the next* to come.

> You wait for the milestones you have been craving-

> *your first kiss, high school, supposed freedom, and limitless adventuring.*

> How naive we were-
> *innocence at its core.*

An aesthetic lore comes with believing aging would bring something more-
> *so much desire in the sea of opportunistic dreams.*

> A leisurely waterbed cultivated for daydreaming of *the next.*

Inspirations of the heart manifested within me of the life that was yet to be.

> The dreams were not restricted to my thoughts at twilight-

> I would run off to escape within the solacing rooms within my mind.

In the car, on the playground, in the classroom-
> I was imagining of what it would be like to live in the beautiful mansions,

> which surrounded my eyes' view.

> *The next* that came with have my own family and an SUV-
> *the dreams felt realistically in queue.*

> The smell of warm cookies on a fall afternoon,
> for my children to come home to,

> just like how my childhood friend's mother would do.

Never in my dreams did I see-

> the mortgage, the heartache, the eventual broken home-
> *or that the cookies were really frozen to bake.*

> *The rose-colored glasses kept me sheltered from reality's wake.*

That is the harsh reality of the rose-colored glasses-
what is real is not always revealed to the masses.

Often the dream is interpreted differently than actual reality.

The friend that has everything she wants,
has a mother she never sees.

Just waiting for the day to come-
the yet to come.

It is but a dream hundreds of miles away.

You blink and before you know-
it is your 15th birthday.

Then your 16th and suddenly it is your 21st-
where is the next that is accompanied with a finish line and fireworks?

So often the next come out broken.
Heartache, rejection, close calls, harsh words, total jerks-

what about the fireworks?

When did the tempo change to the symphony of life?
When did the rose-colored glasses turn to grey?

When did time move beyond giving me the expected dreamy *next* good days?
Is Father Time playing me?

Last time I checked my grandparents were 83,
not 92.

My dog was still young,
with so much energy to exude.

The girls I always knew were a trip down the road or a phone call away,
the time zones had not changed-

and I was without understanding of the true pain of begging someone to stay.

In a blink of an eye everything changed-
I am 25.

Where has gone the first quarter century of my life?

I never noticed my mother's age or a change in my father's pace.

I did not know the losses brought on from my feelings for him,
or recognize the time lost chasing on a whim.

It was all but a dream back then-
my heart yearns for the slow stillness again.

Honey Wheat

Honey Wheat-
　　　　words filled with sweet attachment,

　　　　accompanied with sentimental empty promises-
　　　　punctured broken dreams.

Burbank rose-
　　　　realistic dream occupying the living,

　　　　or just,
　　　　lucid reality?

Movie marathons-
　　　　moving across the TV,

　　　　tell me your thoughts-
　　　　the real ones.

　　　　Open your emotions,
　　　　and empty out your trauma trapped inside.

Instead you escape through the pictures that play across the television screen.

　　　　You see,
　　　　I see.

　　　　Clearer than 20/20 vision,

　　　　spoken or not-
　　　　I hear you clearly.

　　　　Your human nature for some reason,
　　　　comes easy for me to read.

Cling to me then moving on-

　　　　once again you cling,
　　　　I can clearly recognize there is a pattern going on.

Where has the time gone?

　　　　The further we move forward,
　　　　the more distant you become.

I miss the man I once loved.

　　　　Little did we know woman's mind led astray,
　　　　acquainted for the loss within our love.

I know the love never left.

The loss was in our motives,

misunderstandings,
misdirection-

mopping was the result.

Reaching out eventually because we were fed up.

We become unabashed of what the heart wants-
wishing to go back in time.

To keep moving forward,
felt like a crime.

'Can we go back to a different time-
together?

Tangle the present wisdom and knowledge-
knit the fabric of our lives back together?'

To do things right the first time...

To do so——*is not life.*

Let us pray for the chance to somehow make things right.

Let us pray for the opportunity to relive a time of honey wheat-

wonderfully warm,

unbeatably healthy,

enjoyably sweet,

appreciatively welcoming,

to a place where childhood dreams come true.

Technically-

both physically,
and metaphorically,

me and you.

We can only move forward,
forget the factious.

Faith and forgiveness are what can fix this.

From Entity to Individual

My camera is in your possession,
        but that is just one of the things you took from me.

When I implied borrow,
        you heard for the taking.

When I insisted on sharing,
        you coveted for the snaffling.

I failed to recognize the competition I did not sign up for,
        until it was blatantly laid out in front of me.

The things you borrowed were really moving into your ownership,
        and any attempt to open myself up was refired as shots-

        my thoughts,
        feelings,

        and shortcomings,
        were recycled into ammunition.

Bullets of pain were flying at me.

        Inappropriately utilized,
        yet appropriately organized.

When I found some bit of strength you would orchestrate games with my mind.

        Second-guessing-
        gaslit heart professing.

I hid behind the walls of my broken heart,
        convinced there was no option in expressing.

You further conformed my shortcomings-
        I was shut into a box that you made just for me.

        When I found some bit of strength to take glance outside,
        my heart was sidelined.

Shut in and constrained into believing I was wrong-
        wrong for the convictions and feelings that played in my heart and mind.

        'Your actions speak differently.
        How can you love him?
        Do you not recognize our one-of-a-kind connection?'

Little did you know I walked this line once before,
        for a boy I held onto that I had little to no genuine care for.

The bindings were marked with the desire for a loving relationship that signified more-
        and the man I wanted was spiritually broken.

Yet somehow the significance was on me, as your token.

You put me high on a pedestal-
  when I said something about it that made you angry too.

  I was your weekend lover-
   something to fill your calendar.

   But when I wanted to orchestrate an outing,
   we had to double check your planner.

I realized that my life and yours were not aligned-
  when I still thought of him you did not think that was right.

Yet when you went to bed,
  I was not the one you slept next to at night.

You got to have what you wanted while my feelings were tossed to the wayside-

  so long as the proprietorship was on your conditions,
  I signed off to your volition.

Did you see my reluctancy?
  The man that loved you wanted nothing more than his girl to be happy.

That bargain cost more.

  The bill did not fall on him or on you,
  but on my broken heart too afraid to lose.

The fear of losing a friend was real for me-
  it seemed like a trawl to you.

  You desired to have the best catch,

  to gain another medal to hang on the walls of your mind-
  and the lure's strings were attached to me.

Like a puppet I moved to your instruction.
  Never was it me first but rather your wants,

  and I was left to deal with the repercussions,
  because loss was something that I knew too well.

No matter how swell,
  the honeymoon always ends-
  with relationships, life experiences, and friends.

  And even if I do not lose the person,
  there is some erosional bend within the dynamic fabric of our lives.

The inflated cost requires emotional currency to cover the price.
  'Do I wager the loss of my friends and my support in life?'

  I have only recently learned that the extra fees are not right.

Give me my camera back I am not looking for a fight-
  I am slowly regaining my energy, and I'm coming to claim what was taken of mine.

Isaiah 40:29

He gives power to the weak.

He increases the strength of him who has no might.

Dolly's Story (I)

They treated me like toy,

      as they used me to fill an emotional void-
      a playful escape from the pain that haunted their minds.

A mental distraction,
      from the lesser-favored circumstances of their lives.

They shared me and they shared me well.
      They would take turns using me for their emotional spells.

Like a toy I served a purpose-
      my capabilities did not go beyond my conditioned performance.

When I was tossed aside the excuses were justified-
      I held limited capabilities that life had priorly programmed into me.

To read and read between the lines-
      they could not find the time.

The ability to express myself was not listed in the instruction manual.
      Regardless, they did not seem to care.

They continued to try to use me,
      and assumed when I wanted to play.

My lips and brain never knowing what to do or say-
      they would lift me up and move me *this and that way.*

      I would just hope and pray for it to end right away.

My heart did not align with my passive actions,
      and I felt betrayed by them and by myself-

      tortured in my mental prison.

Like a doll I was limp-
      my brain made me feel like a total gimp.

At one point I enjoyed the game when it served as an escape and passive aims-
      being someone's favorite toy can make you feel special that way.

Eventually it became too rough-
      my heart grew sick of it all sure enough.

      with evolving clarity,
      any appeal was removed.

But the others still would exude-
      assume.

Dolly's Story (II)

My mouth had been further sewn over with every undesired sexual exposure.

It started out of naivety in adolescence before I even knew them-
yet the experiences only grew worse as I got older.

The accompanied fear of loss weighed heavy on my mind,
and the failure to gain any proper closure continued to set in-

giving the emotional turmoil permission to replay,
over and over again.

They would never read nor listen,
then repeat the same games from the beginning.

When I tried to act out beyond my capabilities,
they refused to read my facial expressions,

interpret the brokenness in my heart-
let alone psychoanalyze or listen.

They carried on if any attempt to express was just a figment of imagination.

I cannot expect everyone to have the mind of a shrink-

but with every failed attempt my mouth was further stitched shut,
eventually so thick I was unable to get anything in or out.

My eyes had been sewn wide open,
more evident than ever of the horrid houses I had to play in.

I eventually just started to give in-
the only love I knew was an act of sin.

I withered and decayed-

I could not eat,
I did not sleep.

'Is that not what dolls do anyway?'
It was all 'pretend play.'

To just be alive was to thrive-
anything else was not an option.

My mind blockaded the life I was living,

a mentally numbing escape to a world of delusion kept me from quitting-
disassociating from the continual remorse I felt inside.

This is the result from having little to no control and lack of voice over my life.

67

Dolly's Story (III)

I was a slave to the games of desire and lust-
    nothing more than a doll that they would occasionally care for.

A fawn lost in the woods of Grimoire.

Just because I could not speak,
    does not presume I was not hurting in my core.

I was screaming from the depths of my heart,
    and fighting to escape the bounds of my mental prison,

    that locked me into my physical situation.

The key was lost long ago-
    and sometimes I think they knew.

    The seam ripper was nowhere to be found,
    but no one worried about that too.

They continued to move my body as they pleased and stitch over my mouth.

When things seemed like they could not get worse-

    the earth shook,
    swallowing my situation from the core.

I thought I was done for-
    but I was rescued by the grace of God,

    I was removed.

    Through time and effort by the Holy Spirit the stitching was taken out too.

I was provided restoration and assurance,
    through His words that took away the clouds of blue.

    That is how the doll that could not talk is now able to tell her story to you.

2 Corinthians 1:3-4

Blessed be the God
and Father of our Lord Jesus Christ,

the Father of mercies
and God of all comfort;

4 who comforts us in all our affliction,

that we may be able to comfort those
who are in any affliction,

through the comfort with which we ourselves
are comforted by God.

Ivy

Innocent love, that of a dream.

Venit vero sumnio.

You were cultivated from-

> *youthful,*
> *beautiful,*

> *pure-filled love.*

Molded from memorious laughter that is hallmarked by blissful times-
a seasonal period I hope and pray never escapes my mind.

A byproduct formulated by the window of the soul,
in twinkling contrast to the darkness of the night sky-

and as warm and welcoming as the glistening sun,
that is complimented by the late summer breeze.

Superbly supreme.

Rescripsit-
it was rewritten.

Infeliciter-
unfortunately.

Everlasting in my heart,
in another dimension of time,

another life-

the hopeful possibilities are locked away,
along with the flashing memories that made the butterflies excite.

Where the stars align,
I will point you out by your paternal twinkle in your eye.

When we meet again,
my angel-

Ivy Marie.

The Dream of an Eccentric Playwright (I)

It all started out with my childhood best friend, Hope.

A parallel universe,

almost deja vu-
wraith.

Her sister drove us to get fast food in her jeep.
We were then met by another friend.

Let's call her B.

From the restaurant we went to a toy store,
where I witnessed a boy rig his register.

He appeared as an innocent adolescent,
but his character bled with distrust.

The register barely full,
magically filled with 400,000 dollars,

that he stole-.
          well, gave away.

Was he a thief,
or Robin Hood that day?

Mind you this was all still a dream,
but it did not stop there...

Hope and I transported to another store,
where we were met by two other girls.

Their disposition ruminated in intimidation,
which sparked deep regret inside me.

I never really understood why-
maybe it was simply the look in their eyes?

The girls talked of home body piercings,

Teenage angst (rage).

something I knew of too well but,
it left my head rearing.

why was that?

Then two of my present girlfriends emerged,

along with a portal that we gazed into,
where we saw a group of girls hard at work.

It made me sick.

Employment required subjection for a price.

My one friend knew of the business very well,
she said they have one back home-

in the sunny state of bleeding hell.

'where dreams come true.'

71

The Dream of an Eccentric Playwright (II)

Then in a flash of an eye I was lakeside.

I was much younger.

Some man was attempting to use ice skates,

but the weather presumed-
it was not the time or the place.

I sat in the sand in my white dress-

I looked up and I saw him,
from the corner of my eye.

The timeline was at an earlier stage of life,
before we ever met in the waking life.

At a pavilion with his family,
it was the boy I loved from the beginning.

I walked up and said, 'Hello,'

I tried to talk to him,
but little did I know-

the dream kept repeating but before it would,
the reset would be marked by a transition,

to a house full of sisters eagerly retreating.

First the home was set in modern times,

the girls were older,
and at different stages of life.

In the modern day there were three bedrooms,
and one of the sisters inherited the plot-

trademarked by a stone fence
covered in vines.

And when the period moved back in time-

it was the 70s' and the third room,
was no more than a sitting place outside.

With each flash between biomes,

I saw him,
followed by the house,

and with each repetition-
the house moved back in time.

The sisters at one point were not women but girls.

The grandfather clock functioned as a radio,
and the girls gathered around.

They searched for the perfect station-
to make use of their time on the low.

A Poetic Pilgrimage-Isolation Season II

Their mother would not let them listen-
to the station they tuned in on.

                                        But she was gone.

Reading the room,
the fun had just begun.

                          The song 'Goo-Goo Muck' came out in 1962.

                          The girls of all ages were enthralled,
                          with the energy that filled the room.

They danced freely in a line around the living room,
embracing the break from routine gloom.

                          The dinner party they were having-
                          was of no concern when they were dancing.

With each time I saw him,

I would walk up and say *'Hi,'*
and he would take my hand and we'd walk.

                          We would compare lunch boxes,

                          a flirtatious talking point for children-
                          then our hands would interlock.

Walking by his parents and family,
whose ages were before the present time.

                          I do not know where we would go.

The sweet alternate realities,
that formulate in my dreamscape.

                          He always seems to find his way in,
                          my true love from the waking state.

Blue Christmas (I)

Our love had blossomed from early spring,
through summer into fall.

The year was 2018.

I looked forward to spending the holidays with you,

until my dreams turned into-
        harsh reality.

What was full of butterflies and childlike wonder-

        turned into misunderstanding,
        and rainclouds of thunder.

The crashing dreariness of my heart,

catalyzed by the menace of miscommunication-

        since the very start.

The gossiping and the lies,
even the truth was hidden-

or so you thought.
I turned a blind eye.

But then somehow it came back on me.

This brought on a painful spree-

of love and loss,
and love again.

I went to the botanical gardens-
striving to bring about some cheer within.

But as I walked amongst the holiday spectacle,

I was only reminded-
        I was alone.

Everyone seemed to be accompanied by a significant other-
        cheerful and merry in holiday splendor.

That is what the holidays are about-

spending time with loved ones,
and hearing joyful accounts.

All I wanted for Christmas was you-
        but I would lie.

If you asked me what I wanted for Christmas,
I would mutter something materialistic.

No amount of retail therapy could fill the empty void-
        that you once occupied.

Regardless I was left feeling blue-
        I fell to the wayside.

The Christmas before-
    I was melancholy.

2017's sadness transmuted from my dream career
not amounting to what I envisioned.

The Christmas of 2018 I lost my love.

On the outside-
    I was smiling.

Seeing couples kindling left me screaming-
from the inside.

Do others expect me to be happy,
during the jolly season of holiday glee?

Then the holiday passed,
and I heard from you.

You apologized and rekindled-
    we attempted to start anew.

But the pattern ensued.

Blue Christmas (II)

Every birthday.
Every holiday.

It seemed like something would happen-
    deviating our relationship.

It became an unspoken tradition,
    that we would celebrate-

on a furthermore belated date.

Every birthday,
and every Christmas,

people ask me what I want,

where my heart screams for your presence-
    only to be given something more corporeal.

I just smile and say thank you for what I am given.

At least it is something tangible,
    something real.

Empty promises are something I know all too well.

My soul was fed with emptiness-
    like it is a substantial meal.

Sequentially I withered away-

like I was living on a diet of air,
    and rice cakes.

I have tried to regain what I once had and more,

before the soulful sickness,

and the looming sadness-
    vacuumed my life from my core.

This is a constant battle,
    a raging war-

within the walls of my mind,
    and the desires of my heart,

that only God can save me from.

I would be lying if I did not admit-
    my heart still maintains hope for you.

A never-ending desire to reap the reward,
    of everything we went through.

I hope and pray we make it,
the way God intends us to.

Philippians 4:6-7

In nothing be anxious,

but in everything,
by prayer and petition with thanksgiving,

let your requests be made known to God.

7 And the peace of God,
which surpasses all understanding,

will guard your hearts and your thoughts
in Christ Jesus.

Spoiled

What once encapsulated my interest,
has crushed my heart.

Desire mixed with a poisonous decanter,
turning into a homogenous mixture-

it was bound to be spoiled to begin with.

Spoiled it has become.

Proverbs 27:1

Don't boast about tomorrow;

for you don't know what
a day may bring.

A Letter to Her

I used every excuse in the book to justify the ways you moved-

      that you were a misunderstood creature,
      whom prejudice was placed onto.

You appeared to move so slowly,
      so gracefully-

      basking in the sun which accentuated your outer beauty.

A snake seems harmless until it is latched on,

      suffocating-
      refusing to let go until its victim's life is gone.

      Your nature nor your color forewarned me of danger's dawn.

You are a manipulator-

      a liar,
      a thief,

      a deceit.

To the eye you appear innocent,
      but I have learned what is visible,

      is not all there is to be seen.

Following the devil's work,
      your intentions revolve around the theme *'to mislead.'*

You speak words of confusion,
      followed by words of hurt and spite.

You acted to destroy,
      and set fire to everything that is mine.

      Everything that was good,
      that had some meaning to me,

      swallowed that which brought joy and happiness to my life.

You cannot partake in self-injury.

      Rather your anger projects outwardly,
      as the potential ardor must go somewhere-

      right?

The naked truth has been evinced by Newton's laws of energy-

      bitterness brews hotter and more acrid than stale coffee.

One of the many Jezebels I knew-
slyly you continue to move.

Your pride plays tricks on your mind-
truly you are confused.

I used to look up in admiration to you-

joking of the foxy mischief which permeated your playful disposition too.

The games seemed so innocent,

until the stakes grew,
and grew.

You were more than a playful fox,
but a self-driven snake in disguise.

I fell victim to your slithering,

sneaky,
conniving ways-

like others have too.

Before it happened to me,
I thought it was no more than a wise tale.

A misunderstood set of circumstances-
truly I believed I understood the way your personality enabled you.

You slowly stalk,
looking to jealousy suck dry-

the goodness,
the fruitfulness,
and the happiness,

in others' lives.

It is never good enough-
what you have.

You had to go and take what was once mine-
what was once theirs.

So full of hatred and full of spite-
the stalking predator that sneaks through the night.

The curse that overcame you-
from letting the devil rule over the actions your life.

Dream to Nightmare

Renovating Minecraft worlds-
when the simplistic realm,
was within constructed bounds.

The once understood world,
expanded beyond our comprehension.

Sipping strawberry milkshakes,
at the informal place we found.

Our milkshake dates became fewer,
and far between.

Swimming in between traffic,
on a timeline all our own.

Driving together turned into-
a scary dissociative dream.

Repping Ralph Lauren-
clothing that matched your cologne.

Your clothing never changed,

but the disposition you wore-
did not stay the same.

Preparing breakfast together-
made everything taste better.

Breakfast seemed to remain true-
conforming me to a state of hygge.

Working on projects,
in a cooperative environment-
that encouraged each other.

The simple pleasures
made up for animosity.

Sharing newfound knowledge,
we shed deep-rooted enlightenment-

Those nights I still shared with you,
working side by side-

or so that is what we perceived.

now darker than before,
a reminiscent taste left me dewy-eyed.

We agreed on a lot of things-

It was now a wager for peace in exchange-
to relive the sentimental experiences again.

like envisioning where
our future home would lie.

Both could not coexist-
a reconstructed plot of 'Pet Cemetery.'

When it came to sweets-

I liked apple,
while you preferred pumpkin pie.

Some things could not continue,
the exact way they once did.

Everything could not be the way I wanted-

Before and after,
a whole new chapter.

neither of us were fully in control
of the narration.

With a bite of the apple,
in a blink of an eye.

The timeline was no longer mine...

Ours.

But was it ever ours to begin with?

The Safety of Slumber

I find myself sleeping more than I once did.

In my slumber I am gifted with your presence.

A nostalgic dream come true-
when I awaken it leaves me feeling blue.

How I miss the man I once knew.

I look forward to the rest I receive.

It sweeps me away from this heart-wrenching reality,
and takes me back to a safe place,

*A dimension where you and I are still aligned-
an artificial dreamscape of deja vu.*

A place where hurtful words do not persist.

A place that is without trauma and the broken promises-
without the 'what ifs.'

My heart misses you so.

I wish my dreams would come true.

Indigo

Our love was indigo.

Deeply dimensional and abundantly rich like the sea-

it never ran dry,
and was always overflowing.

Warm purples and dark blue hues,
which complimented the calm nature that I felt-

from adorning my presence in you.

Quietly tucked away,
like the time of day that is brought about in the earliest morning sky-

wisdom outpouring,
majesty-filled,

indigo.

Why did the dawning sun have to rise?

I only wish I could freeze time.

Hate is a Strong Word

I hate that I felt like I could not share my deepest insecurities with you.

I hate that I trusted my pain over the potential of the healing process to ensue.

I hate that I fell victim to my senses above my heart.
I hate that my relationship with you fell apart.

I hate that my fears became a reality,
but I do not hate what it has proven to me.

I hate that it had to get to this point,
and I hate that I felt like I was led to disappoint.

Disappointing myself and the child within me-

the circumstantial kindling fed by trauma,
kept unfavored situations brewing and boiling.

I hate that I was right when I thought you could not handle the truth.

I hate that our complicated upbringings created the brokenness inside me and you.

Yet there is so much beauty in the originality and the rawness-
the dexterity that drives the passion of creativity.

I hate the misled directions that occurred in our lives-
the wrong path that we turned down that only led to strife.

Will we recognize the damage we have caused-
that self-inflicted pain from stabbing old wounds only creates fresh scars?

I hate that we have been separated.

I hate that time exists and persists,
and I hate this limbo feeling of waiting to pick back up,

what is-

what always has been,
and what always will be.

I know I showed you 'Spirited Away,'

do you realize you are always with me and I with you,
that we have brought each other to this point?

I know you think of me as I think of you.
I do not care what others have to say.

I know you miss me too,
and you miss the love that we once knew.

John 16:33

"I have told you these things,
that in me you may have peace.

In the world you have trouble;
but cheer up!

I have overcome the world."

A Letter to My Younger Self

How could it be 2023?

I still count the passing days that I find myself missing your heart.

It has been a long while since I felt your presence-
an indescribable comfort which permeates from your essence.

Time has passed for so long I cannot even count.

Every time I see nostalgic tribute to the once was of childhood,

I think to myself-
about the young boy I once knew.

The boy I admired before our time together sprouted,

and flourished-
the way it once did.

The memories I hold dear are like cherished photos.

Mementos trademarked with engraved descriptions written on the back-
embedded montages in my mind.

Priceless.

It is as if I am flashed through a time capsule embedded in a distant reality,
that was not so long ago.

To a place I never even experienced-
an artificial deja vu.

I feel like I hold the memories of your childhood for safekeeping-
even the parts I was never even a part of...

The memories where I was no more than a distant observer,
or the receiving end of a storyteller.

My father asked me what I wanted for Christmas today.

The desire for any material object was clouded away,
by a desire no monetary value could ever equate as an equal exchange.

My heart is calling out to you-

to the boy,
the man,

the love,
I once knew.

All I wanted to receive is the experience of your soulful spirit staring back at me,
with those beautiful brown eyes full of life and hope-

to see the genuine smile I have not witnessed in so long.

I want to experience the laugh I remember,

that is accompanied with the conjoined squinting eyes,
and irreplaceable sparkling smile,

that comes autonomically when you feel joy-

the desire to genuinely witness it just one more time...

I want to hear your jokes,
and see your smile.

*I can still hear your voice echo through the halls of my mind,
where the photos are hung up in a tribute to a different time...*

All I want for Christmas is something I have not seen in a long while.

I want to capture more precious memories for the hallmarked hall.

Every physical thing I ever could have comes and goes.

The pure pleasure of a loved one's presence is a treasure-

branded within the human DNA,
and tucked away,

within the fabric of time and space within the soul.

I always dream of the good and bad the times we shared,

*the potential ones we could have had-
the artificial deja vu.*

Even the alternate realities of the past-
I miss the possible chances we almost had.

*I wish I could step back in time-
tell my younger self,*

'It is alright.

*That boy you love,
he will love you too.*

*Just follow God and never look down another path.
You are worthy of the love you feel inside.'*

Taking Back What is Mine (I)

I am disgusted with the power I have given to your name-

> frustrated with my racing heart,
> that is triggered at the thought that you are within fighting distance.

I become anxiety ridden-
> overcome by weakness that knocks out the strength in my knees.

> *I try to maintain my breathing as my vision's coherence escapes me.*

All because I know you have walked away scotch free,
> from the mischievous tricks you have pulled.

My senses overcome by what can be seen-
> *the devil's sly leverage sieges my energy.*

He reminds me of the unsettling guileful games you played on my mind,
> *and words you spoke to create damage within the landscape of my life.*

Never once did I willingly work to corrupt what was yours,
> *but you still plotted corruption against what was mine.*

You recruited those I cared about most to your army,
> turning them away from my standby.

> *Were they ever really my friends if they were so swift to form opposing sides?*

> *The devil knew what he is doing,*
> *and what he continues to do.*

> He was the one to enroll and recruit.

The words I spoke with concern towards your name was just poor attempt-
> *an attempt to have an ill-equipped therapist fix the cracks in my life.*

> I searched for the cure to mend our relationship-
> *a possible remedy so I was no longer fighting in strife.*

I was misguided and ill-informed-
> *something the master deceiver is trademarked by.*

You can never be friends with your therapist,

> *and more importantly-*
> your friends are under-qualified and ill-equipped at being an arbitrator.

It was a six-year emotional war of give and take that started out soft,
> *but soon enough greater wagers were at stake.*

> He knew the battle he was brewing *but we never envisioned what would take place.*

90

It was never about us to begin with-
it was a fight between darkness and light.

He continues to try to remind me I was just a steppingstone in your life.

A fill-in for your once recent absence of friends-
turned into a job description of occupying an emotional void,

full-time,

something I related to.

I did not recognize the similarities at first-
the desirous qualities we expected from the other's company.

For I just wanted a friend that did not leave me,
when they got a glance of something supposedly more desirable.

A theme in my life I knew all too well-
since adolescence.

He knew the emotional warfare he was plying.
I guess we were both looking for acceptance.

But in the passing of time what you wanted no longer aligned with my desires.

I did not want a friend who would leave,
and his reminders fed a lack of confidence to that emotional fire.

The longer it continued the wager to maintain the relationship grew even higher,
which dug deeper into my preexistent adolescent agony,

thus,
eating away at me slowly.

I later discovered-
the relationship reinforced your childhood's parental emotional tragedy.

Yet we did not stay away-
we continued to wound each other almost every other day.

To the naked eye nothing seemed wrong,
but in our hearts sung a familiar, sorrowful song.

The Mental Killer (Taking Back What is Mine II)

Furthermore-
> I felt uncomfortably copied in both traits and hobbies that you admired.

When jealous frustration overcomes me,
> *I try to remind myself it was often the wrong model you took to follow.*

In the past I tried to look for answers and find my own way,
> and you would slowly string along with every step I would take.

> *We continued to lead each other down a trapdoor enclosed hallway.*

You liked what you saw-

> copied and pasted,
> redrafted just enough to get away with plagiarism.

Your version left out my scars,
> that left me searching for answers.

The redraft did not include the broken heart,

> that left me running away as an escape-
> *like an emotionally deteriorating cancer.*

The hurt that made others think,

> *'Was it really that bad?*
> *She must be weak or exaggerating.'*

You took *the pretty stuff,*
> and threw the rest to be buried in the dirt-

> *the why,*
> *and the how.*

You molded my search for peace into your aesthetic couture.

> But I know your own pain,

> saw your desire for acceptance,
> and need for assurance-

> which made you only want more.

It all just seemed like a fun aesthetic somehow,
> at least from the outside that is what you made it seem.

But little do you truly understand the damage my choices created,
> and the mutilation that took place within my heart at its core.

Learning as you are living for the first time-

> there is bound to be flaws and errors,
> *yet that did not seem to be applicable to me.*

I was never allowed to mess up,

> *not with my parents,*

> *not with him,*

> *and not with you.*

You placed me on a pedestal-
> *a poster child to look up to.*

With each error and change of direction-
> *input would always emanate behind every move.*

> Leaving me to defend my thoughts even when,

> the fear,

> the pain,

> the inexplicable feelings-
> *made me incapable.*

I was supposed to be perfect,
> an encyclopedia with all the answers,

> and because of that,

> my flaws deem me unacceptable and vile to many people-
> *especially you.*

> *It was like my self-assessed lack of self-worth came true.*

My world lacked grace from the people that surrounded my view,

> this only further enforced the idea I could not back away.

> I could not change-
> from what I grew into.

I saw your hurt and tried my best to help,

> but you do not remember the attempts,
> just the failure-

> *trauma truly is a mentally inflicting killer.*

I am Praying for You (Taking Back What is Mine III)

I never informed you-
> your attempts to alleviate my pain did not make me feel better either,

> even in the imperfection-
> I was just thankful to have a friend.

> *Like always,*
> *I chose to hold it all in.*

I was thankful to have someone-

> that when I would call,
> they would answer.

> *Even in my brokenness,*
> *I would just take what I could get.*

My dependence fed my fears of loss,
> enforcing my inability to speak up-

> *the cycle was continually embraced in my relationship with you.*

Even when I tried to-
> my worst fears came true.

> The cycles continued,
> and continued-

> *breaking me down further from any independence,*
> *any assurance that I had left.*

My life's consistent theme was of people leaving me for something better-
> something that lied ahead.

> The devil knew what he was doing-
> planting seeds of fear and doubt in my head.

I have come to learn it is better to lose what does not fit,
> *and it is okay to shed old skin.*

You can have my friends,

> *you can continue to try to copy aspects of my life-*
> *at this point I am mostly old news to you.*

The fascination and sparkle died off-
you got enough ideas of what you can use,

rewrite,
and redo.

There are probably others you look to for exemplary design,

until you gathered enough inspiration,
and move onto the next idol in your life.

I have tried to warn others of the trickery that floods our humanly lives.

I am imperfect yet-
I continue to try.

I am learning to no longer fear the pain,
nor feel the frustration-

that the devil pawned off with intent to destroy my innermost light.

Those days are through.

I am learning to rely only on God and myself,

to allow reconstruction,

and allow goodness to overtake my life.

I hold forgiveness,

it was not all you-

it was the recruiter that latched on to your mind,
giving you commands that you followed through.

I am praying for you.

Untitled

I beg God for a second chance,
      but at this point I am on my 15th.

You count the xs by my name-
      the mental reminder fills me with grief.

I know there is better out there.

      Better situations for me to find,

      more anchored situations to call home-
      but predictability bores me.

I rather face the rocky waters,

      and go where my heart calls out to,
      than dwell in an insipid biome.

What encapsulates my heart has overtaken my life-
      13 years I spent in love with you.

      I did not comprehend what that emotion truly was,
      until you were in proximal view.

The art I once admired from afar fell into my possessional dwelling-

      and now I will fight to reclaim what has been repossessed.

Did I always know,
      or did the devil play me hard?

      The master deceiver pulling every trick card.

I waited for 13 and I would wait for 13,000 more,

      but this is not a Christina Perri Song,
      life on earth is deemed short.

Yet I could have the world handed to me,

      superficially-

      what should be prioritized is miscued.

In a world preoccupied with status and wealth,
      all I want is love and good health.

      All I want is happiness and peace-
      all I want is for your spirit to be back in its rightful place.

I beg and I cry to God every night-
        to return my love back in my life.

My dreamscape is flooded with my true desires-

        since I was 12 years-old,
        they have only transpired.

For God made man-
        Adam and Eve to be one and one on earth faithfully.

        I recognize where we did not follow that model correctly.

        My therapist even assured me that she has witnessed your love for me.

I know we have had our shortcomings,
        we both have done each other wrong-

        running and making decisions from our senses,
        rather than listening to wisdom's warning song.

I miss you.

        I love you.
        I just want you home.

I would trade every earthly possession for the return of the repossessed love,

        that intensely drew on our souls.

Psalm 56:8-11

You count my wanderings.

You put my tears
into your container.

Aren't they in your book?

9 Then my enemies shall turn back
in the day that I call.

I know this: that God is for me.

10 In God, I will praise his word.
In Yahweh, I will praise his word.

11 I have put my trust in God.
I will not be afraid.

What can man do to me?

Four Words

I cannot sleep.

Four words.

> Tears in my eyes.
> Insomnia and pure frustration.

Wanting an instant reply-

> anxiety preys on indecision.
> *Anxiety keeps me frozen.*

You are probably sleeping.

> Glancing at my notifications,
> hoping to formally ignite-
>
> our occasional twilight communication.
> *Maybe even an invitation.*

My stomach in knots.

> Maybe it is just-
> the time of month,
>
> or it's pure anxiety?

Now it is 4 A.M.

> The gut-wrenching deprivation,
> the fidgeting-filled aggravation.

I try every remedy-

> retiring to bed early,
> after extended self-care.
>
> Opening my northern window,
> even during winter months-
>
> with warm weighted blankets,
> and water on standby.

I choose watching movies,
as an attempted remedy.

> To cure my difficulties-
>
> *difficulties resting my eyes,*
> *and my tired mind.*

That was our thing-
> impromptu coincidental cinematic themes.

> A familiar nostalgic comfort,
> that is bitter-sweet.

I refuse to rewatch-
> ones we've already seen.

> Even at first glance,
> I taste the reminiscence.

It is now 5 A.M.

> My descriptive mood is-

> mad.

> I cannot even retire,
> to a numbing slumber,

> to the time capsule-
> filled with your memory.

Is God playing me?
> *It simply cannot be.*

> I pray out asking-

> 'Oh please,
> let me!

> Let my eyes close-
> my mind contract peace.

> Must I lay awake?

> If so,
> speak wisdom to me.

> Do I give it a few days,
> or do I reach out in melancholy?'

Four words-

> I am thinking of,
> I am in love,

> insomnia is better spent-
> (with) you.

Psalm 102:7

I watch,

and have become like a sparrow
that is alone on the housetop.

Reality Awakens Me

I should know better by now-
>dreams do come true.

Not the maladaptive daydreaming-

>the trap laid through the act of fantasizing,
>that is twisted into whole-heartedly believing mirages,

>but the dreams that are prophetic forewarnings.

I distract myself in the waking state with your smile,

>I hold onto each memorable flicker like time is running out,
>as if it may be the last time I am graced by its glimmer.

>The unconscious programming feeds distraction rather than truth.

We are on different paths-
>but I ignore the facts that my instinctual senses perceive.

>'Anyone can be saved.
>Everyone is worth the redemption.'

Ironically it is my nightly slumber that awakens me,
>to the truth that the incessant cycles bring on self-inflicted mutilation-

>that I have once again willingly locked myself into a maladaptive prison.

The reality is that we are separated.

>We were once on the same trajectory,
>but you find error in my changed direction-

>that makes two of us.

I cannot speak on spiritual knowledge anymore-
>your filtration creates blockades for any premising.

>The security system runs and rebuttals shots of self-assurance-

>pride.

Yet I continue to stand,

>ignoring the rebuttal,

>placing hope into the fact that actions speak louder-
>fortified against consequence.

I awaken with tears in my eyes.

'Oh! How your soft smiles and sweet words put me asleep-

but only for a short time.'

While asleep I was awakened,

these seemingly good moments are short-lived,
and remaining in them will envelope my body in poison.

It is only going to get darker,
the longer I remain in the maladaptive dream turned nightmare.

I mourn the love I lost-
that I long to have again.

How I wish to awaken to the timeline I hold onto within my head.

O.C.D.

Overcome by mental stress-
I just want to be enveloped in peaceful rest.

I am full of deep regret-
a result from my shortcomings consuming the wiring of my mindscape.

Yet again-
it is a virus.

Cleaning.

What was supposed to be meditative,
and fulfilling,

turned into a gut-wrenching chore-

one that lashes out,
bruising you from the core.

A side quest that threw me into a brick wall.

Distress pounds from the prison of my chest.

Nothing looks acceptable,
even if I am trying my best.

Decisions.

Midnight whore-

fulfilling the graveyard shift,
orders aplenty.

Employee of the month,
or a used doormat on the dirt floor.

When the sun comes up you are reminded,
they are just a customer that your heart throbbed for.

They do not think twice about you-
even if they flagged you down.

Requested by name-
you fulfill what they came looking for.

Your vessel is no more than a host for parasitic OCD,
and a body to fulfill devilish fantasies-

working two jobs,
while the emotional tax is greater than the payout.

God help me.

Protection Program

You have placed me on an isle out of protection,
spirited away to a different dimension.

A place trademarked by immaculate sunrises,

pink clouds,
gentle laughter,

and overwhelming peace.

I once called a dystopia of distraction and confusion my home.

An environment branded by civilization full of noise and running movement,
but now I find myself quietly sitting alone.

The noise of others has been replaced by the gentle breeze of Your creation,
a pulling wind that moves west beyond that place.

It carries Your whispering assurance filling me with Your peace and grace.

I have been whisked away by Your protection,
transmuted by Your endlessly enduring love,

from a place that once seemed utopian-
when my vision was impaired by drugs.

The drug of confusion,
powered by emotionally jarring illusion.

The drug of fear,
enforced by self-led control.

The move was not easy on my heart at first,
but only when I look behind me do I find myself melancholy.

Those are the moments when I must remind myself the true story that did unfold.

I cannot sugarcoat or forget,
nor rewrite history-

doing so consequentially ends in the repetition of tragedy.

The story is not over,
every falling action brings a worthwhile ending.

Even if it is not what one was expecting,
we are incapable to assume every detail the Storywriter is plotting.

Be sure to watch the *'Story of Life'* intently through to the final curtain closing.

I promise you what He is planning is far better than what you may be enduring.

I Need to Let Go

Why did I look back?
>Nothing has changed.

>You use me as your toy.

I was overcome with Christmas joy,
>at the thought of spending the holiday with you.

>But I should have known it is all a ploy-
>an emotional decoy.

I have changed,
>but you remain the same.

>Self-centered,
>and absorbed by ego-

>dictated and controlled by pain.

I know not to look back,
>but in the distance of my past, I hear your call.

>My body is overtaken by emotionally jarring memories,
>reminding me of what I love.

Strings attached-
>'Does anyone know where the scissors are?'

>You tuck them away in a drawer-
>only you know where they lie.

>So that when the time comes you can cut me free-
>after you are done using me.

Like a child,
>I am at the mercy of the one who I look to with innocent wide eyes.

I already know the ending of this story-
>it has been spoiled for me.

>It is hard to look at a situation differently,
>when you have experienced it tediously.

But human nature puts hope in the heart of the beholder-
>that is why in your domain I am tucked away.

My eyes do not trust what they do not already know-
>the hope for something better was broken long ago.

I need to just give it to God,
>and relinquish my need for emotional control.

Job 22:21-23

"Acquaint yourself with him,
now, and be at peace.

By it, good will come to you.

22 Please receive instruction from his mouth,
and lay up his words in your heart.

23 If you return to the Almighty,
you will be built up,

if you put away unrighteousness
far from your tents."

The Monologue of an Artist

If a girl shares with you her poetry-
she is permitting access to a vault of precious documents locked in her heart.

Take heed-
she has translated the language engrained on the walls of her inner-most self.

As she writes she is knowingly providing a Rosetta Stone.

A bridge for an outsider-
revealing a transcription of emotions that one cannot simply decode on their own.

A manuscript holding recordings of her beating heart and active mind.

The collective is armored away and bound within the safe that is her body,

and further glossed over by her amiable expressions-
she wears a disguise from the outside.

Someone would never truly know what lays behind the masked archive.

Even if they were to attempt an assumptive educated guess,

of what lays enclosed behind her decorative expression,
that serves as a vessel of protection,

the reality is-
that the dossiers are tucked away far from the onlooker's eye.

For when she sheds light on the language within her heart,
she is also revealing the innerworkings of her mind,

life produces, and catalyzes-

the process,
that translates to afflatus projects.

Creative genius, they call it-

locked away behind the raw bare bones is the comprising of her spirit.

There is fragility to the precious system of inner light that continuously burns inside.

She holds onto it as it provides the passion to create-
the rib cage is the tabernacle holding the ever-present light of the Spirit.

The fire never ceases,
even when the temporal world consumes her body to dirt again.

Her thoughts live on within the framework of space and time-

a longevity outlasting the material she records on,
that is eventually recycled again by the earth.

Inspiration is the everlasting successor of the artist.

If a girl reveals her work,
        acknowledge with intention-

        like a child that displays their masterpiece on the fridge or wall,
        there is reasoning behind their choice audience upon presentation.

        Acknowledge it-
        accept it.

        Take the time to digest the work and to listen-
        for a majority have overlooked,

        a 'that is nice dear' and a quick glance at most,
        but who cares to give true genuine attention?

        Who is aware enough to recognize the unique God-given light inside them?

        No two hearts beat the same.

If a girl shows you her art-
        she is giving you a glimpse into her mind that ignites her creative eye.

        The practice of her mental process,
        which digests each step she takes in her life.

        The result of imprinted experiences that stay with her,

        long after they move behind-
        the recordings of the beauty captivated by her detail-orientated eyes.

The attention you exhibit gives her understanding if you really care-
        care to hear of what genuinely lives inside.

        Art is in the eye of the beholder,
        but do you care to try to read between the lines?

Where is the Altruism?

The ones I trust most,
    are the ones who hold a knife to my throat.

    An ultimatum reminding me-
    I can never have both.

You are taught to be expressive and speak your mind,
    but this setup is implemented as evidence when persecuted on trial.

Be kind,
    but do not be naive.

Do good,
    but do not let others step on you.

Listen,
    but also speak up.

Be understanding,
    but make sure your guard is up.

My world when surrounded by people loses saturation with each day.

    The mixing of mixed signals turns from vibrancy to muddy brown.

I try to maintain the beauty I see on the colored TV,
    but reality reminds me it is only a scripted display.

My heart of optimism is disappointed,
    causing my spirit to slowly decay-

    I lose my hope in humanity a little more each day.

I desire nothing more than good people around me.

    I know we all sin,
    but where are the ones who are trying their best wholeheartedly?

    Everything seems to be a selfish aim,

    my energy is exhausted-
    I guess I am to blame.

Forever a target for practice,

    a doormat,
    a fill in space-

    but never the one someone's world is intentionally built around.

    This leaves me to question, *'Am I the self-centered one?'*

I am scared to love again,
     I am scared to let anyone in-

     even my family employs waging bargains.

     A conditioned premise that my world is established in.

It is nothing new to me,
     and I am no longer taken by surprise.

     I desire to find the emergency exit,
     but every time I do,

     I am hurt far more than before-
     a pain greater than when I was behind the door.

     My distrust is the result from an ongoing pursuit of believing in a better world.

I crave the softer life,
     and I choose to remain inside-

     where I am silently bruised away from the bystanders' eyes.

A sickening familiarity-
     knowing what to expect is safer than contracting the illness of unfamiliarity.

     The dog eating dog world that I want to believe is an untrue reality.

     I find myself alone again.

III

IN HIS HANDS

III

Do You See the Gift?

Do not mope over what God does not deem as right.

Do not focus on the appearance of lost time,
nor mourn the opportunities that lay in rearview of your memory,

they move past your frontal viewpoint-
beyond your control.

Fixating on the past restricts the ability to fully see what displays in present light.

When we mourn the changing of our shadow,
we are facing away from what is freshly illuminated.

This allows the mind to be occupied with a search to conjure,

prior memories,

past conditions,

familiar situations,

into the current reality-
resulting in present opportunities passing by.

A lack of a watchful eye,

or maybe the culprit of one-
all depending on the viewpoint you stand upon.

A blinding abyss of only wanting what we know to be true-

an unappreciation for the now,
and a lack of desire for the new.

He is trying to give you a present.

Do You See the Gift?

You will not know what is inside until you face Him,
and you open it.

Do You See it?
What are you waiting for?

We may not know what is inside,
but I can guarantee there is goodness instore.

There is always beauty within a surprise.

I urge you to face the light,
and to keep an open mind.

Like Moths to Light

How Good Is He?
That the God of creativity and perfection also created you and me.

That He fabricated us from the likeness of His essence,
filling our vessel with purpose-driven incandescence.

With every breath He puts movement within us-

He hands it over with trust,
His direction for application is like a weathervane hit by gust.

He desires for us to shine our light,

whispering gentle reminders that,
'Everyone was made just right.'

He individually distinguished us since our adolescence-
having planned for us before our physical existence.

Nothing is more luxurious than a one of a kind-

down to the number of hairs on our head,
and the beating in our heart,

we were all made 'just right.'

With His master signature labeled 'mine,'
He embedded ownership over mankind.

We are His children,
young and old.

He cares for us,
throughout the entirety of the life we hold.

From the day we are born until the day we pass,

and even beyond-
He is with us.

On our best days and our worst,
He is there to remind you of your worth.

That He has a plan for you,
as He has written.

That He forgives you,
regardless of the circumstances given.

That He desires for us to fulfill our purpose,
and be in His presence.

That He gives us the freedom to be with Him,
    without the use of coerce.

We were made in likeness to Him,

    and our freewill for better or for worse-
    is not on a whim.

    Our experiences bring wisdom and the chances to live a closer life with Him.

Life experienced on this earth is only a fraction of His goodness-
    He desires for us to be able to experience Him within His fullness.

    It's easy to forget this truthful declaration in a world pushing for separation.

It can seem so much easier to find our own way,
    until we unknowingly take the wrong path and are led astray.

    Lost we become,
    just trying to find our way home.

How good is He-

    The Shepard does not abandon His flock,
    He will always seek you out and offer direction on where to go.

    Not forcefully but lovingly,
    He sheds light on the way home.

Home is where the heart is,
    and our hearts are with Him-

    the providence,
    the restoration,

    the peace of home is what His true nature is.

He knows every thought and feeling that makes its way in-
    that fills your body to the brim.

He understands your individuality,
    and asks you to give your hopes and fears to Him.

When we do so-
    He will replace our sadness with joyful hymns.

Encouraging us to gravitate like moths to light.

What we want and need-
    is not far from our sight.

When we have God,
    He will not let us down.

He will always provide a map marking the way-
    a way trademarked with providing your life true restoration today.

Psalm 119:105

Your word is a lamp to my feet,
and a light for my path.

A Guide for Navigating Snakes (Information)

A snake remains in camouflage to the naked eye.

To be able to point out a snake from afar is an adroitness task-
        they conceal in between appropriate colors as an attempt to mask.

        They hide from predators who may try to attack,
        and stalk prey from their den's crack.

        Watching.

        Waiting.

Many times,
        it is not until we are within close proximity do we see,

        where they were hiding,

        and analyzing-
        you and me.

        And even then-
        it is hard to tell exactly where they'll be.

They may camouflage in plain sight,
        blending in with their surroundings,

        and when you get close-
        they will bite.

Without awareness,
        we can be left fully regretting our steps of carelessness.

        When we get bit,
        it is a result of poor perception-

        a result from forgetting where we are stepping.

We are in their domain,
        must I remind you.

We can fall for the trap that was laid,

        all a snake needs to do is wait-
        in its perfect hiding place.

So now that I forewarned you,
        let me share with you some life-learned tips on navigating snakes.

Psalm 140:1-4

Deliver me,
Yahweh,

from the evil man.

Preserve me from the violent man:

2 those who devise mischief in their hearts.
They continually gather themselves together for war.

3 They have sharpened their tongues like a serpent.
Viper's poison is under their lips. Selah.

4 Yahweh, keep me from
the hands of the wicked.

Preserve me from
the violent men who

have determined to
trip my feet.

A Guide for Navigating Snakes (Application)

Here are some tips for navigating snakes:

Cover yourself with truth.

Be full of awareness,
        especially when you are walking in their home base.

The wilderness of the mundane world,
        is full of hidden snake dens where slithering beasts lie waiting to uncurl.

        Bearing righteousness also means bearing wisdom and truth.

Move with awareness.

If you move too fast,
        they may try to bite as you walk past.

Watch where you cast stones,
        most snakes are defensive and will jump at you when you throw.

Educate yourself on the snakes of the world,
        so that you can know where to expect them-

        help yourself navigate and avoid those which creep from the underworld.

        The word of God is a tool that uncovers the truth.

Stand firm and walk in peace in all you do.

        If you remain in stillness they cannot see,
        an isolated body is a form of protection by the power of God's divinity.

A slow life is best really.

        In the swift heat of it all,
        the cold-blooded beasts' movements are relentless,

        which can leave our defensive bodies tired and restless,
        when faced with the circumstances.

Take on the helmet of salvation to defend yourself from the inside.

The devil can try to send fear to your mind,
        but what he will not tell you is that he cannot see beyond the outside.

        He can only hear you when you speak out loud.

        Like when you are sharing words with others,

        and being a loudmouth.

Watch your words,
>they can be used as a weapon to plot your downfall.

You would not tell an opponent your every move-

>treat the world like a game of chess,

>and God is your coach-
>telling you which strategy and next play is best.

Shield yourself.

>Guard your mind,
>and guard it well,

>to withstand the attacks the devil will try to sell-
>on the doorstep of your mind.

>He does not want you to know he cannot see what is truly inside.

Temptation is not what it looks like,
>it is no more than an impulse buy-

>short-lived,

>and often bringing on more regret and debt than it is truly worth.

So, I tell you one more time to avoid the snakes and embrace the armor of God-

>that will guarantee protection to your heart inside.

Ephesians 6:12-13

For our wrestling is not
against flesh and blood,

but against principalities,
against the powers,

against the world's rulers
of the darkness of this age,

and against the spiritual forces of wickedness
in the heavenly places.

13 Therefore put on the
whole armor of God,

that you may be able to
withstand in the evil day,

and having done all,
to stand.

Settles the Score

The Fairest Judge is on my side.
He knows exactly what lay inside-

my dreams,
my shortcomings,

even the lies.

The lies the devil fed me-
the lies that left me deprived.

The temptations that overtook me-
some as deep as the roots of a willow tree.

Weighed down,
entangled-
for so long they hung over me.

I trusted in Him to set me free,
and He always will hold that capability.

My trust in Him made the work easy.

The lies I once believed weighed me down to the point I could not breathe.

Pure anxiety-
through the practice of piety,
He has shed light on the hidden deceit.

Exposed-
no further room to grow,

now what suffocated me,
no longer has a chokehold.

My feelings of doubt He casted away.

My struggle with depression He had come to slay.

My lack of self-worth has been replaced by restoration.

He has brought joy to each day regardless of the circumstances given.

For that reason I stand tall and restored-
because of my God who loves His people through the journey of it all.

He holds my hand through the hills and the valleys-
He makes a way.

He makes the path secured.
He will always settle the score.

Let It Shine

What is light,
        but an absence of darkness.

Before the antithesis,
        there was solitary.

    Separation under free will stretching the spectrum-

    widely.

But in a universe constructed under the bounds of creation,
        the circadian rhythm beats to a drum like photosynthesis.

    Slow in darkness,
    and full of motion in light.

    The sun never ceases,

    we only change position-
    like the light in us,

    that is beyond our manufactured jurisdiction.

    Ordinally passed down by the birth right of Adam's predecessors.

There is something about the look in the eye-
        the window of the soul that sparkles from the housed Spirit inside.

    Further driven by the relationship of the Son.

In a world operating under the circadian rhythm of physical light,
        the Spirit works beyond the construction of earthly timelines.

I once was so asleep not even the light of day could awake me-

    bound by a sickly feeling comparable to scurvy.

But the existential depression was eliminated,
        and replaced with an eternal source of renewable energy-

    a source that will forever exist beyond my needs in this physical body.

Like the sun,
        I am the Creator's vessel-

        for the power He sources through me to bring good things to the world.

He Who Raises People from the Dead

If it were not for the wise poets in my life and the Holy Spirit-
    I would probably be six feet below the surface.

They never let me forget my purpose-
    reminding me that my sufferings hold worth within.

The needed patience bears intention,
    for Christ sufferings bore the greatest burdens.

He faced every trial with discernment and joy,
    showing us how to properly employ.

Employing our God-given usefulness-
    following the proper steps promises fruitfulness.

That does not mean we will not face backlash and scrutiny,

    hurtful comments,

    and tests pertaining past baggage and bigotry.

He asks us to give it all to Him.

    When we are feeling weighed down,
    feeling like we could drown,

    within the treachery of this world of tests,

    the necessary application of hard work,
    even when surrounded by a world of sin,

    He reminds us-
    'this is a team effort,'

    God provides strength within.

    All we must do is turn and call to Him.

And He will even take on some of the load,

    because of His love-
    you are never actually alone.

    So just ask.

My paternal father reminds me that pressure makes diamonds,

      and because of these words,
      I do not fear what lays beyond the horizon.

More importantly I do not fear,
      because God's truth speaks to my heart's listening ears.

When we seek,
      we shall find.

When we ask,
      we will get answers.

Worshipping the things on this earth is a choice,
      but ultimately wealth comes from the Father's rejoice.

      Hearing the words, 'well done, my good and faithful servant,'

      resulting from His words and our actions being convergent.

Regardless of what you see from the outside,
      I have been remade on the inside.

The dirt has been removed-

      I have been set free.

Now that I am shown how to move,
      there is no dirt on my feet-

      the Holy Spirit keeps me clean.

2 Timothy 4:18

And the Lord will deliver me
from every evil work,

and will preserve me
for his heavenly Kingdom.

To him be the glory forever and ever.
Amen.

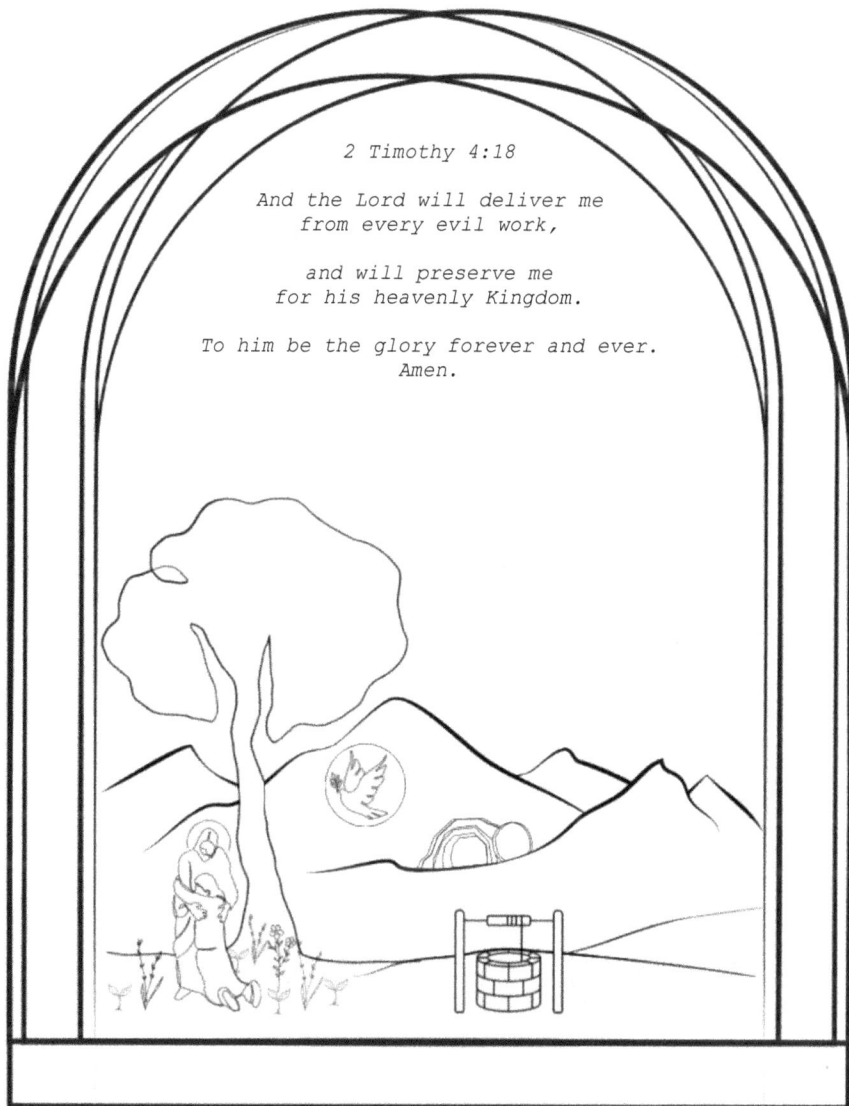

To Love Me or To Love Me Not?

I question why God gave me such a deep unconditional affection for you-
the current lack of a happy ending causes unceasing emotions to feel so cruel.

I am reminded my unconditional love is but a fraction of the Father's love for us.
It is unfathomable to explain-

My feelings inside that are beyond physical expression,

rattling in my body-
as they consistently remain.

The psychological effect physically rotting my brain,
and the frequent reality shock feels like freezing rain-
I am shaking.

No matter how much hurt you cause-
my love for you continues to live on.

I know God's love is far beyond human comprehension.

No matter how far we move from Him,
or if our course of action becomes vile or cruel-

He is still reaching out with loving affection,

like a hardworking fisherman-
He never tires and He never gives in.

He will not forget about us even when we curse against Him.

Vulgarity stems from our frustrations and limited understandings-

we combat against Him,
without understanding why He lets the storylines play out the way He did.

And I have come to learn and come to know,
the test is not about if I can end up happily with you.

It is really a test of finding more love in my heart,
for The One who encourages me to grow-

whose love surpasses any of my humanly emotions that may ever ensue.

He whispers to the heart,

'Do you love Me more;
do you trust enough to endure?'

The story is not over.
I promise you goodness is coming,

full of His perfection,
and bringing much more beyond our own understanding.

Isaiah 49:15-16

"Can a woman forget
her nursing child,

that she should not have compassion
on the son of her womb?

Yes, these may forget,
yet I will not forget you!

16 Behold, I have engraved you on
the palms of my hands.

Your walls are
continually before me."

It Is All About the Soil (I)

I used to love to look at the flowers in bloom.

In admiration I dreamt of the sequential colors that supplementarily ensue-
how tall they would stretch to.

Admiring the different hues that matched the pigments of my own soul-
and those I secretly wished were stained along the walls of my heart.

Adoring the ways the floret danced and moved,
as if God was playing for them their own personalized melody.

From a distance their beauty incapsulated me,
but the closer I grew towards them I realized-

the flowers were not growing right.

An unfortunate result of their environment-

the weather the seasons bore,
and the wretched soil,

stunted the growing bloom.

I did not realize until I spent a long time in the meadow,

and even then,
I would turn a blind eye.

Assuming everything would get better methodically-

in divine time.

I registered premature budding was underway-
the closer I was in proximity.

The flowers once spoke sweetly coos,
that drew me to their once bountiful blooms.

But now only painful cries for help could be heard-
as beauty turned into doom.

The withering flowers attempt to let out a scream one last time-
for the suffering that inflicted them was not of their own demise.

I had to remove myself from the environmental gloom,
protect myself from the turmoil that ensued.

From afar,
        anger-filled petty insults are now all the best they can do-

        throwing cheap shots like childhood bullies in middle school.

In attempt to make themselves feel better amongst the pain,
        as their bodies go into shock from the air that is cool.

The flowers speak to me.

I am still in admiration of their beauty,
        regardless of the imperfections that are continually brewing.

There is beauty within imperfection,
        that is actuality.

        A poster child is no more than an impractical reality.

They ask me when I will grow up,
        but nature's mirror is itself-

        emotional immaturity,
        poor development,

        fumbling cause and effect that results from their environment,
        continues to feed a stunted bloom.

The soiled beauty catalyzed by,

        outpouring insecurity,

        resentful bigotry,

        talking bitterly-

        the planting in poor soil.

It Is All About the Soil (II)

They raised up,
    like a rose covered in thorns.

Beautiful from afar,
    but they made me bleed to the touch.

Hearts black as coal,
    which matches the absence of light in their soul.

Depleting essence,

    in all the wrong ways,
    they search for a source of incandescence,

    just to keep their body from losing its essence-

    parasitic.

The drought inflicted soil and absorbed rage has sparked ensnaring flames-
    spreading all where they are permitted to go.

    Impacting their heart,

    like a raging fire,
    they carry the burning desire,

    to constantly spread igniting pain-

    emotional arson.

The attempt to attack,
    with the assumption I am dried out like them-

    thinking their works of the devil will overtake me too.

Their unkind words blazing with rage,
    like a hurricane they attempt to spread a psychological monsoon.

But it is hard to set fire to what is nourished-

    green,
    healthy,

    full of potential to flourish.

The nourishment does not come from the beautiful colors,
    nor the ability to stand tall,

    but rather the balanced soil that replenishes my soul.

Filled by the holy waters of the Spirit,
not dry and sparse like the southwestern deserts-

not deserted.

They can try to set fire,
but it will not work.

They can cut the heads off my bounty,
but it will only make room to grow more.

When evil comes to attack me at my core,
my roots stand firmly nourished-

and will always endure.

I have been planted in good soil by Him,

and He shines down on me,

with an outpour-
my Lord.

I will endure because of Him,

I dwell in safety.

Psalm 1:1-3

Blessed is the man who doesn't
walk in the counsel of the wicked,

nor stand on the path of sinners,
nor sit in the seat of scoffers;

2 but his delight is in Yahweh's law.
On his law he mediates day and night.

3 He will be like a tree
planted by the streams of water,

that produces its
fruit in its season,

whose leaf also
does not wither.

Whatever he does
shall prosper.

Haute Couture (Classes)

Handmade with love-
        I peruse the aisles of second-hand items.

In actuality-
        some have been passed around more times than you can count.

Numbers of them have been passed around for their-

        third,

        fourth,

        fifth time,
        trying to find a fostering home.

No consumer will ever know that though-
        or maybe they can tell.

Some garments are cared for so delicately,
        you would not be able to distinguish they were ever owned previously.

Each owner passed the garment along gently from store to loving home to store-
        these are the ones that were always gently cared for.

        These are the lucky ones like the lucky souls in this world.

They move from one relationship to another,
        one stage of life to the next,

        from care to care without any wear to their silhouette-

        never having been stretched thin,

        never tattered,
        nor stained,

        never torn,

        or altered,
        or maimed.

Then there are the garments that are messy.

        They are put through the wear and tear,
        and sometimes not mended properly.

In some circumstances this happens overtime after being with many good partners,
        they age like fine wine-

        a discoloration here,
        a stitched patch there.

        They have been a part of many memories-
        their markings are tattooed souvenirs.

142

Other times the luck of the draw places them in a less ideal situations every time,

      battered and bruised,
      easily disregarded,

      used up-
      discarded.

Regardless of their beauty,
      they become stained and not tended to correctly.

      Often worn down faster than they should-
      stained by the battleground of the world that they were recruited into.

Then there are the ones who are locked away and trapped for so long-
      locked away in admiration and safekeeping.

      Left to do no more than collect dust when they were fabricated to be-

      recognized,
      admired,

      utilized.

      They were created to exist as a perfect piece within someone's life.

Instead they were hoarded away,
      and trapped for a long time on end-

      like a jewel only visible to the beholder to examine,

      They covet what they fear will be snatched from underneath them-
      jealously fearful of another eye's admiring *their* possession.

Sometimes they are just held to have-

      hoarded away under superficial appreciation and little sediment,
      lack of attachment even.

An absence of memories makes the divinely crafted garment mature into old news-
      detached we become to the garb that once sparkled in initial view.

      The one we just had to have-
      the one that was clung onto.

Then the day comes death do they part,

      or not-

      the garment is released when the coveting is through.
      The appealing rush of it all wore off.

True appreciation means both functionality and care-
      the garment may not be tattered,

      but the pungent color is not as prominent as what was once there.

Haute Couture (Veritas)

Each soul is like a garment of clothing.

The memories made and the milestones lived woven into each-

> pattern,
> texture,
> and style.

> Some are fully embraced and cherished-
> and others are overlooked.

Each soul is sparkling and uniquely designed-
> fabricated to bring joy and some type of purpose into others' lives.

The garments are like the hearts of the world.

Whether-

> tenderly cared for,

> battered and bruised,

> torn and forgotten,

> tucked away and hidden.

All were uniquely made to be,

> recognized,

> fully embraced,

> and appreciated-

> upon initial passing view.

What was made for me,
> is not always what was made for you.

But each creation holds-

> functionality,
> beauty,

> and purpose,

> in this world it was created into.

Take gentle care of the souls,
> even the ones who are but only a seasonal garment to you.

Luke 12:6-7

Aren't five sparrows
sold for assaria pennies?

Not one of them
is forgotten before God.

7 But the very hairs of your head are all counted.

Therefore don't be afraid.
You are of more value than many sparrows.

C.W.

Created in His image-
creative, empathic, and kind.

Ordained with a giving heart of gold,
a God-given gift maladapted by earthly conditions-

compensating for a void within community,
both from *his* present and past.

The devil tried to profit from the imperfections of earthly tragedy.

You see,

the master deceiver tried marginalizing on work within other campaigns-

a broken home,

unjust suffering,

sexual exposure,

a loss of friends,

and a distant fatherly figure.

A tactic he has been using since his downfall,
creating catalyzed havoc on God's beloved people.

The world's lies fed to him like a poisonous fruit-
a tragic rewrite of Snow White.

Never did *the man* intend to make the wrong choice,

as *he* battled between the world's propaganda fed in *his* head,
and *his* good heart's voice.

But he was carefully watched over by The Almighty Protector,
making sure his heart never fully lost its light.

You see-

God is a loving Father who protects with love and discipline-
the tough love experiences were implemented to refine *him.*

His hand constantly over him like guardrails protecting him.

The man's life was not to end as his God-given purpose was not finished.

Next steps were always given,
      even if *he* wanted to completely give up and give in.

      God knew his strife since the very beginning and kept him close,
      even when his worldly vision made him feel all alone.

      He says there is a special place in His heart for those who suffer most-

      patience,
      never anger.

      more patience,
      and more opportunities.

Opportunities to open-up *his* heart to what the devil was trying to have *him* miss-
      through a dissociative sleep.

      A detachment of who *he* was created to be-

      one of God's children,
      made unique and perfect as He designed *him.*

      But God set *him* apart,
      with a direct motive to revive *his* heart-

      at his own pace.

      The revival was not a forced race,
      but rather a gentle journey marked by a consistency of love.

Revival provided for the brokenhearted-

      he is reminded of *his* purpose,
      and *his* energy restoratively renewed.

With every experience God never left *him* abandoned,
      cultivating a living testimony of loving meaningfulness to awaken within.

      He awakened from the dormant sleep the world tried to restrict him in-
      his spirit renewed.

      A sleeping Snow White awakened,
      and detoxed from the worldly poison *he* once digested.

      The heart of gold restored to its former,
      to how God perfectly designed-

      creative, empathic, and kind.

2 Corinthians 5:17

Therefore if anyone is in Christ,
he is a new creation.

The old things have passed away.

Behold, all things have become new.

Faith as My Shield

Is it a test of faith,
or wishful thinking?

Is that not what faith is?

The belief in the unseen-
the yet to be.

Faith is a convicting comfort found in having assurance in the yet to unfold-
an overwhelming sense of peace that is found within the process.

When the world feels dull and the odds appear stacked against,
when I am left guessing what is to come and when-

faith provides the answers,
it burdens the purpose,

it promises there is progress in the process-

faith cheers that character is built through unexpected sharp turns,
and builds a road ahead to eventual success.

Fear comes knocking at the door of my mental space,
intending to wreak havoc on the personal property labeled as 'mine.'

It attempts to make its way to the innerworkings of my heart,
from the doorstep of my mind.

I will not let the battle go beyond the barricade.

There is barbed wire of truth laid,
sandbags of assurance create a blockade.

God's truth reigns down like grenades,
targeting the false ideologies,

the passive apologies-
anything that is not true love.

The truth is more than a spiritual weapon.

It is more healing than a well-versed paramedic-
more effective than a specially curated elixir.

Truth provides instantaneous concrete stability,
and gradual solutions that lead to certainty.

I tell you the next time fear comes waging at your doorstep,
call upon faith to deter and conquer the warring fret.

Matthew 10:16

"Behold, I send you out
as sheep among wolves.

Therefore be wise as serpents
and as harmless as doves."

Symbiosis

She reminds me of him.

The familiarity stems beyond their physical characteristics.

A deeper resemblance than what can be seen,
        beyond their grey hair and green eyes.

        The real coat they wear is trademarked by love and loyalty-

        strong and cunning,

        caring and curious,

        courageous and wise,

        watchful and loyal,

        loving and beautiful.

They do not need to speak,
        in the silent moments their disposition proudly displays their intentions.

The famous saying rings-

        'Actions speak louder than words,'

        as their nature embellishes character greater than I can vocally exude.

The God-given souls in my life that I am adorned to watch over-
        or maybe it is the other way around.

I cherish their comforting company and never-ending loyalty.

She can be skittish,
        and it only reminds me of his intelligence and dexterity.

And when she goes out of her way to spend time with me,
        it reminds me of the constant admiration he displayed towards me.

And when I miss him,
        she reminds me of the mission she continues to carryout in his memory.

They are more than just a pet-

        a brother,
        my child.

        Family.

I will cherish my memories from my time on earth with them for eternity.

Genesis 1:26

God said,
"Let's make man in our image,
after our likeness.

Let them have dominion
over the fish of the sea,

and over the birds of the sky,

and over all the livestock,
and over all the earth,

and over every creeping thing
that creeps on the earth."

Echo

Soft pinks whose color match my blushing cheeks.

Smooth ivory which compliments my satin skin.

Belle-colored yellow is what my mother always said I looked best in.

Rich rouge that mirrors my beating heart,
instilling life into my body.

The green stems of vivacious vibrancy,
support the life that stands beside me.

The flowers by my bedside are a reflection,
reminding of the beauty God has placed in me-

beautiful delicacy,

unique perfection,

the well-thought intricacy.

Each individual component flows together in organic composition,
making up a body of harmonic imagery.

At dawn and twilight as I rest in bed,
and all the time that lay in between-

the flowers serve as a mirror-
a reflecting of me.

As I tend to their frailty,
I am reminded of the gentle nature I must show to my own body.

If you care for them well,
they will last long and maintain their vibrancy-

and even in passing,

when they dry the imagery of their colorful life is all you have in memory.

Spirit Seeds (I)

There is a well-known saying that you fall in love 3 times.

He was my first.

I was too young then to decipher the intense infatuation which overcame me,

I now know it was indeed the spark of true fireworks-
the instantaneous ignition set off by love at first sight.

The forget-me-nots were released over the soil then and there.

The spontaneity planted the desire to admire,

admire from afar-
digging deeper.

I desired to see the flowers break through as I would blankly stare-
fearful of ruining the blooms before they were visibly there.

The soil had been treated long before he came into my view,
before anything was placed into my garden bed.

I accepted the fertilizer the world sold me,
comprised of doubt, worthlessness, and worry.

I buried trauma that further malnourished my garden,
nourishing the narrative-

'I was unworthy of the connections my heart readily wanted.'

As a result of their scattering,
the seeds of our love sat in the soil,

a few years later a single flower broke through-

but my worries overtook the plant,
and grew true before the flowers could ever really bloom.

My sadness watered my garden as I solely tended to her.

This resulted in me settling within my second growing season,

while attempting to cultivate in a new direction-
a supposed fresh start.

A seed I planted out of blind trajection,
simply directed by choices to avoid loneliness and rejection.

I hoped for anything to produce fruit and bloom.

The growth was quick but tending to it brought about discomfort,
    like tending to allergy-inducing vegetation-

        hives and a headache,
        an uneasy allergic reaction,

        an overwhelming warning-
        proceed with caution.

        Short lived-
        eventually dug up and discarded.

My third was not for me-
        a similar theme that mirrored my second.

        Comfort came solely from the acknowledgment of sewing something,
        but it was not something I found reward in.

        I still thought about the forget-me-nots every day,
        even as I tended to something entirely different.

The soil was still fertilized by insecurity,
        and as time went on it was further treated with the devil's impurity.

I was just a child full of naivety and insecurity.
        An ill-fed garden bed is what my mind and body came to be.

The plant was spoiled long before maturity,
        and after seasons of stubbornness all that grew was unhappiness-

        I recognized I was without reaping,
        I removed the weed I had been tending,

        and accepted this reality.

        I accepted that whatever was supposed to be,
        would be provided to me-

        anemochory.

Then my first came true,

        my first was him-
        spring came and the long dormant forget-me-nots sprouted again.

The second and third were simply not what was true-
        no more than a weed and an undesired bloom.

        A death sentence and an antipathic weed only bore discontent-

        love cannot be forced nor rushed,
        unhappiness will always ensue.

Spirit Seeds (II)

I gave up and started fresh when the forget-me-nots sprung up into waking view-
were my dreams intuitive inklings that I always knew?

My heart treaded slowly-
fearful to lose what I believed I was undeserving of reaping.

In less than two months the blooming flower whispered,
'I love you.'

A lack of words barricaded by a montage of truth-
that is when reality hit.

That is when I realized my heart had always known,

a knowing of what love at first sight really was,
and the meadow quickly grew before my very eyes.

Regardless of the fear of rejection,
restless discontent was nonexistent in the rooting of our connection,

it was like the peace of being home-
the comfort of homeostasis found as I lay in my bloomed meadow.

The small forget-me-nots multiplied and consumed the spaces of my garden.
The previous clearing gave space for this to happen,

I was without lacking-
I felt both comfort and vivaciousness.

Our love was alive and in the right conditions it quickly grew and spread,
but the dormant seed had laid for a long time beforehand.

The soil was poorly treated from desperately striving to harvest love in my life-
I listened to false propaganda through my years of gardening in strife.

The flowers became tainted as their roots were exposed,

to things that had laid in my past,
conditions that were not beneficial to their growth-

I blindly treated my garden bed in desperation to cultivate something.

The poison had seeped in,
and weeds further sprung up trying to take over again.

I now believe some love is a product of steady slow growth,
while some love is immediate like the arrival of spring's green,

regardless of its velocity-
pure love always lasts through any season that should pass.

John 15:1-4

"I am the true vine,
and my Father is the farmer.

2 Every branch in me that doesn't bear fruit.

3 You are already pruned clean
because of the word which I have spoken to you.

4 Remain in me, and I in you.

As the branch can't bear fruit by itself
unless it remains in the vine,

so neither can you,
unless you remain in me."

Spirit Seeds (III)

The loss of the first seed's bloom broke me more than the second and the last-
they never had a chance.

The garden bed was poisoned from present to past.

I looked for something to bloom since the loss of the meadow of forget-me-nots.

Sometimes I am given hope when they pop back up,
but they have yet to last for more than a month.

I have tried to find beauty in anything that takes growth-
often later I come to learn most blooms that end up here are invasive,

both to the garden bed,
and to the flowers I love most.

Now I have learned that love can also slowly grow even if it lay dormant-
in the right conditions it will not be spoiled.

I have tried to fix the garden on my own,
but I have learned-

some things take the True Gardener's work to mend and grow.

Without light the plants life cannot uphold,

the True Gardener warned me darkness lays ahead,
the longer I try to fix the garden bed-

single-handedly on my own.

Fungus, weeds, and poor soil will persist when trying to cultivate alone.

Without living water,
the roots will dry out and the plant will wither.

Without nourished soil,
my love alone cannot save the garden from poison or stunted growth.

Maybe one day God will tend to the first bloom,
and fix what bolted before it produced genuine fruit.

I cannot dismiss the other works God is doing in my garden-
under the right conditions.

I allowed the world to pollute my garden,
    but He is removing the soil and replacing it with nourishment.

        He has tended to the ground and the branches,
        leaving what He finds goodness in.

For now-
        I must give it up to Him,

        believing regardless of the spirit seeds He places within the garden bed,

        if it is from Him,
        they will be good.

        If I care for the soil as He teaches me,
        I just need to be willing to His providing direction.

Love can grow again as a production of His goodness,
        and I will reap an everlasting harvest.

Conscious Actions

I choose to no longer chase-
a conscious decision that I had to make.

Painfully I have grown aware,
that the game is not 'follow the leader,'

but really a game of cat and mouse-

unfavored,
full of distaste.

And as I move further away,
you come looking for me.

I leave you wondering where I went,
as I am no longer following your lead.

The thing is I would have,
and a piece of my heart still wants to-

the human complex is driven by the repetition compulsion.

Now it is you who is chasing me-
stubborn are we.

I have longed for an end in which we moved in harmony.

The idea of controlling the narrative enabled me,
some days I solely blame my OCD,

but victimization regardless of its validity lacks repairing-
it is without healing.

A title is not what brings about saving.

Wanting the upper hand,
when I always was a step behind.

The more this has continued,
the more exhausted I have become.

It has been a fight between compulsions,
and what God wants.

The more illuminated the circumstances are,
the more the luster is lost.

I no longer look with interest and appeal at the traps you lay-
but I would be lying if I said they do not spark melancholy.

Moving independently takes maturity.

How my heart wishes things could have ended up differently.

It took several tries to refuse to turn around-

to dismiss the sale of known security,
that comes with desirable familiarity.

Yet the sparkle of human interest that once encapsulated me,
that I found in you,

I cannot find anywhere else-
it is gone from view no matter where I look.

I had been left in the dark,
and when I search for the spark what I find is all artificial.

The rare gem of my heart,

the one of one-
is nowhere to be found.

The only light I see is that in the One who created me,

His Spirit,
and the nature of His Son.

I have faith one day I will stumble upon human companionship again-
God only knows when.

I always loved you despite your faults,
but even John bore warning to not bind ourselves to earthly love.

The Waiting Room

The walls are grey here-

> where the ticking clock taunts me,
> and a vacancy of vibrancy is found in my current occupancy.

> *The only diversity I see is that which shines through the windowpane-*
> *but that place seems to be a distance away.*

I always struggled with patience-
> my stubbornness needlessly getting in the way.

> *Things always appear more delightful elsewhere,*
> *where the grass was greener.*

I desire to want what I want under my conditions,
> which has only created blockades-

> *impulsive inclination prompted by belief in instantaneous gratification.*

The walls reflect a grey void of constant repetition and little spontaneity,

> a blank canvas that I so often have left prematurely-
> *only to find myself back in this space suddenly.*

My choices resemble-

> *a circle forcefully rammed into a shape shorter fit for a square,*

> *baking without preheated preparation,*

> *the impulsive purchase made without executive decision.*

> *I faced the consequential shortcomings from anxious impulse.*

I have learned the hard way as I am-

> *restricted beyond further entry,*

> *underdone and rushed before ready,*

> *disappointed by what it has cost me.*

> *The ticking clock always taunts me-*
> *back to square one.*

Something that I have avoided admittance to-

> the struggle with impatience that insistently took root,
> and stubborn inclinations that once had sole jurisdiction of my mood.

> *If only I had more patience.*

My brain employed tricks on me-
    prompting prior conditioning to move on before I was properly ready.

    Like dashing through a test without doublechecking-

    mistakes had been made,
    components were overlooked.

    What could have been avoided was pressured on an unnecessary deadline.

I always dreaded the waiting room-
    the melodramatic normalcy and repetition quickly became old news.

I have found myself here more times than I like,

    in trial and error yet,
    I chose similar choices every time.

Human nature is conformed to known normalcy,
    that is why choosing outside of what is known takes God's guiding lead.

My mind has fixated on the countdown until I am out,
    with the dreamy desire of the greener grass that I felt separated from.

    Like a child dreaming of weekend plans yet to come,

    ignoring the present school lessons,
    that will eventually reemerge back into relevancy.

    I raced out the door only to reenter with Monday's arrival-
    I once proceeded like nothing was to subsequent Friday's leisurely escape.

I am learning to treat my times here with the value that it has.

    What once struck me as boring,
    has given me peace.

I now see the potential and benefits of the blank canvas making up the four walls.
    I am not bound to a finished story as my life is continually unfolding-

    restoration,
    knowledge,
    peace,
    and preparation.

Do not rush to finish when it is not a race,
    value the time you are given in your waiting place.

With every misstep I have ended back here,
    but it is now clear-

    I am growing within safety.

Romans 5:3-5

Not only this,
but we rejoice in our sufferings,

knowing that suffering produce perseverance,

4 and perseverance, proven character;
and proven character, hope:

5 and hope doesn't disappoint us,
because God's love

has been poured into our hearts

through the Holy Spirit
who was given to us.

Latibule

My best friend reminds me-

if she let me sleep outside forever,
I would do so freely.

A lush meadow as a plush pillow-
a real-life Sleeping Beauty.

There is an everlasting comfort I find within the expansive fresh morning air,

a void where worldly schedules are not found-
a living journal where my thoughts and dreams linger.

The enchanting chimes' echo can be heard dancing playfully in the esoteric breeze,
delighting me with whimsical charm,

like a beloved character of a fairytale story-
welcoming me back again.

I invite the nightly air through the entrance of an open window,
where my secluded dwelling expands as she is breathed into.

Filling my body and my vessel,
elevating my spirit elsewhere-

gracefully whisking me away in peace.

Nature's beloved charmer.

The early twilight breeze,
brings about a heightened state of homeostatic peace.

The trail I am guided on smoothly rocks me to sleep.

Even in an awakened state,
it whisks me to a tranquil place.

As I look to the north at my neighboring hallow-
the orange streetlight and mature trees are fortified in resting place.

In a waking dreamland my scrapbooked reflections lay.

A place for reminiscent recalling and reflecting always remains.

Montages timestamped within the view of my windowpane,
a memorial reminder of the once was and is-

some things always exist,
and some things resist change.

Fireproof Faith

'Give it time.'

My pastor reminds me what my grandma taught me-
while the world tries to tell me otherwise.

It seems too good to be true.

I pray to You wholeheartedly-
I pray for him.

Tears stream out of my exhausted body.

I pray to maintain direction,
that I do not lose sight again.

My friend tells me I am like Ester.

The resemblance comes as a surprise to me.

Men flock and they gawk-
flattery is nothing more than a sweet breeze.

Like sweets at a bakery temptation is quick to spoil.
The desirous pleasantry holds an expiration.

I would much rather stay single,
and place my bets on him every time.

It is your embrace that does not grow old to me.

Your kisses that cross my mind-
a role I found that you can only humanly provide.

'Shall I go,
or shall I remain?'

Even when the odds appear stacked against,
why settle for loose change when there is a chance-

to strike gold.

How beautiful it is that a God
who saw a need to create me,

also saw necessity and beauty
with a world that had him.

'A world pictured without you,
is no more than a world filtered through a blue hue.'

I blink and we have been here a quarter century.
I cry out hoping his spirit will soon be renewed.

I pray,
I hope,

Time moves so oddly-
impatiently slow and yet somehow too swiftly.

Faith is the force which allows God to work,
for the good of His people.

I place my bets on it every time-
I believe it is God's reassuring voice.

Fruitful Character Development

Once young and on the vine,
 we playfully danced in the sunshine.

Despite the cloudy days,
 our spirits were rich and innocently unblemished inside.

'what will we become?'

 A doctor, a singer, an architect, an artist, a bus driver,

 even a fashion designer-

 the validity of our life choices stretching,
 throughout the realm of our joyous daydreaming.

We grew larger overtime,
 still connected to the vine-

 the days of torrential downpour slowly began to outweigh the sunshine.

As much as we need balance to grow,
 sometimes the soggy soil had caused rotting within the soul.

I joke to you how we are getting old,
 but surprisingly it is you that reminds me there is still time to grow.

 So often I forget we have yet to reach the ends of our lives.

Even when coffee and community has turned to tears and tea,

 when sunshine and scrapped knees turned to overcast days and worry-

 as long as we remain attached,
 there is always hope to remain alive.

 To continue to grow,
 to ripen-

 nothing is experienced in strife.

A doctor, a designer, an architect, an engineer, a singer-
 we must maintain hope in a ripening future.

 God is not done writing the story of His fruitful characters.

170

John 15:5-7

"I am the vine.
You are the branches.

He who remains in me,
and I in him bears much fruit,

for apart from me you can do nothing.

6 If a man doesn't remain in me,
he is thrown out as a branch and is withered;

and they gather them, throw them into a fire,
and they are burned.

7 If you remain in me,
and my word remain in you,

you will ask
whatever you desire,

and it will be done for you."

Weather Forecast

In clear view with the shining sun,
  peace is absorbed as it reigns from above.

  But God forewarned us-
  there will be days when the weather forecast is bound to change.

For a day,

    even days,
    and sometimes seasons-

    the storms will roll in making it feel as though the light has gone away.

    Like weathering rocks,
    we can be broken down in the places that we are bound.

The reign of good days appears outweighed,
  by the rain of the storm that has moved into domain-

    with the cold making us feel further isolated and alone.

But no matter the weather,
  or the time of day-

    the sun remains.

It is the promises of the Father,

    the wisdom of the Spirit,
    and the accompaniment of the Son,

    elevating the soul to a place above the weather faced on earth-

    which we find ourselves on.

No weight is too heavy for the God who moves mountains-
  welcome Him to uplift you with open arms.

Unsolicited Soul Ties

They see a ravishing woman-
a primal recognition for the beautiful body that she possesses.

Do they realize the magnetic allure that draws their attention,
is beyond the temptation of physical attraction?

An unacknowledged enticement for divine bridegroom essence-
a thirsting need for God's presence.

Desirous need for quenching fulfillment,

a resemblance is found in her auric energy-
craving to combat deficiency through the recovery of the missing rib.

A physical bandage for a spiritual insufficiency.

A woman of God's Spirit exuding desire more magnetic than humanly pheromones.

The brain trained by the senses,

what is thought to be intrinsic is instinctual-
animalistic.

An unfortunate dilution by the sensory processes that chain the spirit.

There is more than what is seen by the eye-
a blockade between heart and soul creates a reroute to the mind.

what holds the ability to see the aura of divine feminine beauty?

To see it for what it is,
beyond physicality?

Many are attracted,

but few can truly decipher the current's pull to still water-
they wrestle within the riptide.

Like the moon that she is supervised by,
the power is unknowingly in her hands.

They are not attracted to the woman but to the Spirit of God that lives inside,

pulling the prospectors in,
as they work to hide the shortcomings in their own lives-

denial.

The true connection they thirst for,

the revival-
blindly they search the earth for the everlasting elixir.

A Conch's Perspective (A Conscious Perspective)

Individual life is full of wonder.

As we come and as we are,
　　　　broken or fully intact.

A familiar resemblance to another,
　　　　but never perfectly exact.

It takes an observant heart to see the individuality in me.

　　　　The duality of complexity,
　　　　and unmistakable simplicity.

　　　　The embalmed macrocosm in a microcosm.

Ventral I lay my insides exposed,
　　　　my colors displayed for all who glance my way,

　　　　*if they may-
　　　　their eyes engrossed.*

　　　　My artistic display mimics sun-kissed oranges and pink petals,
　　　　that ombre into a blankness that wraps around my frontal.

One in several billion-

　　　　the color composition,
　　　　the varying size,

　　　　the curvature of shape formation,
　　　　makes me one of a kind.

Even those similar at first glance are not a carbon copy,
　　　　as I was uniquely made in the Creator's eyes.

At this point I remain whole,
　　　　while others arrive as a surviving piece of what they once were-

　　　　fragmentation caused by rough waters and predatory orders.

We flood the sandy earth as we are,
　　　　adorning the white canvas with texture and color.

Fate has brought sunshine onto our core,
　　　　after being ejected from the expansive sea that once bore us.

All beautiful and uniquely designed-

　　　　*just as we are,
　　　　just as we come.*

Some of us stay for a while,
and others arrive for a moment before going back where we came from.

The ways of the water uncover the wonder that is God's observational character.

There is much similarity to me,
and to the souls who walk along the shore He places them on.

Some sit for a while,
and other only a short time,

with all returning to the real home where they came from.

Divine timing,
one of a kind-

in the hands of the Potter who never exhausts His creative light.

Spiritual Maturity

Could it be the developed mentality overtime,
or the repetition of events that broke me?

I used to run with full force wherever my heart was called to-
a 'free spirit' was the defined title for the girl I once thought I so well knew.

Without examination of the steps I took along the way,
I would dream of the disembarked point without second thought of looking down.

The elongated destination appeared pleasing,
until I realized the path was misleading,

It was not enroute-
a misinterpretation to where I thought I would be arriving.

The world is so straight forward until realizing each road leads somewhere specific.

The open meadow is really a maze,

filled with hills and valleys-
home to thickets, potholes, weeds, and snakes, and caves.

The journey cut up my feet and scraped my knees-
the course brought me to a winded dead-end without a sigh of relief.

And stubborn as I am,
I took my stamina and tried again,
and again.

As an attempt to get where I wanted,
the way I thought I knew how.

Sometimes crossing into bounds beyond further entry,
other times looking for a shortcut I could fabricate just for my needs.

That is the problem with chasing specified fantasies,
we run from what is in front of us-

living on borrowed time to create what we think we want and need.

After probably 100 failed attempts of building fantasies on sandy soil,

I opened my eyes to see,
wisdom's compass is not under the jurisdiction of emotion's breeze,

and the window of my biological clock is closing with each tick of passing time.

The opportunity for good experiences were drowned by overconsuming thoughts-
of how to create what I want and the reflection of past whys'?

I refuse to give up rather I choose to lean in.
No longer will I choose to solely navigate on emotion.

God is my tour guide who bears His never-failing compass of wisdom- and my life is a trip.

Psalm 43:3-4

Oh, send out your light
and your truth.

Let them bring me to your holy hill,
to your tents.

4 Then I will go to the altar of God,

to God,
my exceeding joy.

I will praise you on the harp,

God, my God.

Kintsugi

A living example of Kintsugi.

What was meant to destroy me,
has only reformed-

rerouted,

refined,

reinvented.

My delicate body and intricate glass heart-
once blatantly labeled with fragility.

Now I am fortified stronger than prior times,
my emotional being has been transformed,

more beautiful than ever before seen.

The mind's eye holding a watchful disposition,
and the physical body has been reshaped.

*I was once a shell cracked open-
simultaneously stepped on as my contents were fed onto.*

No longer do I allow my body to be preyed upon.

*I have been awakened to my inner strength and beauty,
as what did not kill me has only transformed me.*

The Old Saying Goes

I cannot save you,
but I can pray for you.♡

Gardening Season

I am a vessel-
housed in a flowerpot of undergoing potential.

Fruition is not restricted by my timing,
nor the vase I currently find myself in.

A safe zone for growth and stabilization.

Once a mustard seed of faith contained withing a gardening tray-
my environment is thoughtfully controlled and watched over with care.

I will eventually be planted in a field where my meadow can flourish,
just as I was placed in this vase following my maturing faith taking root.

Time is all He asks for to ensure proper fruition.

I know I am nourished in His hands.

A period of protection for my evolving roots to grow firm,
and for my adultizing stock to grow tall in love.

I am a vessel of God's testament and love.

Knitted Hearts and Soft Smiles

This is for the women in my life-
the diamonds amongst the calloused worldly rough.

For those who continue to let their beautifully particular nature shine amid strife-
they are patented by life's luster and delicately designed souls.

In a world where bushy thorns latch and snag at softly knit hearts-

caught and damaged,
and so often unraveled.

The ones who envelope the undeserving world with warm unconditional love-
while they go to bed cold.

Those who put on an amiable smile-
while emotional pain tries physical destruction in the home of their soul.

To the ones strong enough to see another day-
even when the cards they had been dealt appear poorly laid.

So many have been misunderstood,
and their stories are judged upon an initial onlooking glance of the cover.

Their kindness foreseen as weakness,
their hardships overlooked as mere scars,

shortcomings translated as red flags-
all are judgements that have been mismarked.

The Father made you,
and He skillfully repairs you-

fabricating His intentional creation in a more remarkable piece of art.

You are a beautiful composition of your interwoven earthly testament-
for those who care to read your beautifully comprised sediment.

James 5:11

Behold, we call them blessed
who endured.

You have heard of the perseverance of Job,
and have seen the Lord in the outcome,

and how the Lord is full of compassion and mercy.

The History of a Miraculous Mirage

For so long I found solace in where I was placed-
      concealed behind a boundary of two-way glass.

On the other side of my dwelling were a display of desirous mirages,
      for prospectors to view upon glance.

See not heard,
      that is how I was stowed here-

      my feet bound by preconceived standards,
      and further cemented by the solitude I found in the deceit of it all.

The supposed transparency brought about the realization,
      that who I display myself as is not who I have to be-

      like being on the inside of a powerful cascading waterfall.

Their onlook was shielded from my internal struggles and my innermost dreams-

      all they witnessed and heard were the stories they reasoned,
      like the interpretation of modern art.

      I feared the repercussions of stepping outside the solace I remained in-

      due to worry of rejection,
      and previous mixed reactions to my adolescent transparency.

From an early age people did not take kindly,
      to the bold outspoken nature God placed inside of me-

      I learned to acclimate and protect my fragility.

A fortress of solitude and a mental prison served as a double-edged sword-
      one that I grasped firmly to as it simultaneously inflicted pain onto me.

Painful cries were seen as smiles,
      and struggles were distorted as an effortless dance.

Only when they dared to step close enough,
      press their face onto the glass,

      or dare to dive through the entrance and see-
      the mechanics of the beautiful mess that became of me.

But few have gotten so curious and even in my most vulnerable moments,
      they have inflicted pain onto me-

      I guess that is what I get for trusting someone with another's psyche-
      the confiding bears some degree of liability.

I have worn 100 coats,
        and shed 1000 skins,

        the remains deposited onto the floor of the prison I found myself in-
        until they were no longer.

You see-
        my engraved walls are the only souvenir that remains.

        I purged each piece of evidence from the past,

        that I once held close-
        into fiery blaze.

I am a collector,

        of memories not things-
        I will not be weighed down.

The memories are incombustible,
        even if I want them gone.

        They leave little room for the good that simultaneously transpired.

        History is a reminder that keeps the past from repeating.

I am a secret keeper,

        a memento holder,
        a mental decompressor,
        a dream warrior,

        but to them-
        I am just a girl.

        Viewer discretion is advised.

Aquinas's Riddle

What is homeostasis,
    but a meaningful stride for balance and peace?

Humans search for the everlasting solution,
    to meet their consistently emerging needs.

Just as we find beauty and sustenance in the world around us,

    the fulfillment is temporal-
    no longer lasting than the sand that falls from Father Time's hourglass.

There is a period and place-
    experiences are just a drop of substance within the fabric of time.

Food is no longer after consuming,
    and a night's passing is always followed by morning's rise.

Even the beauty of companionship has a deadline attached-
    two timelines overlap but are never perfectly aligned.

Temporal integration of slipping solidity.

    What is harmlessly good never endure past its scheduled terminality-
    this is the quality of the recycling earth.

We search for permanence in a temporal world.

    Building with loaned materials-
    structuring sandcastles made of dust we carry in our pockets.

    We put pressure on creating diamonds out of sand,
    and conquering the ability to freeze time.

But the concrete nature of the ocean's tide will always wash away,

    recycle-
    and renew.

Spirit's desires are misdiagnosed as earthly wants of permeance.

Selective Minimalism

I have more pillows on my bed,
than friends in my circle-

but in the end,
I sleep alone as I push them all aside.

They are no more than another adornment in my life.

A decorative fixation that I look at with pride.

A charming admiration during the day show little substance,
and lack purpose as they sit on my bed.

When it comes time to find rest,
I lack the room and comfort to lay my head.

At nightfall where can I turn to vulnerably lay my head?

No more than a daylight visual desire,
like those I once held so dear-

quality over quantity is preferred.

Prayer Goodnight

Holy Spirit be with me,
        as I slowly drift to sleep.

Thank you Jesus,
        for this day.

        Thank you Lord,
        for this world you have made-

        for my family,

        Your providence too,

        like my health and sustaining food.

Jesus,
        please keep me close tonight,
        bless me with sweet dreams-

        embed in my heart,
        and dig deep into my life.

You are truly the reason,
        through any and every season.

I give thanks,

        I hold trust,
        You burden Your love,

        You remind me I am enough-
        You are more than enough.

Grace

You bring light into a sleeping world with every step you take.

With sustained awareness you bear sight and warmth with your presence-

> *within every smile,*
> *and each embrace.*

A child of God surrounded,

> *protected,*
> *and aligned.*

It brings joy to watch Him work through you,
> *and witness the mastery of art you paint and present to the world-*

> *I am elated to be able to call you my sister in Christ for a lifetime.*

1221

The birthday blues cycles back once again.

Torturous headache-

> to match my bounded frustration,
> and your impounded soul.

We suffer,
> my heart aches.

> *I cannot help but feel sorry for you.*

An empathic heart,
> and a mediated therapeutic mindset.

A problem solver,
> a solution finder,

> a philosopher just wanting to understand-
> *driven by a desire to restore homeostasis and balance.*

> *I may plant the seeds,*

> *but I am not the project manager-*
> *I have done my work here.*

Worry.

> A captious mind is a ton-filled weight squashing any convincing credibility.
> *Internal affliction eats you away.*

> You find comfort in surrounding thoughts that convince you to remain-
> *within the sandstorm of confusion.*

'Look within,'
> is lost in translation.

The outside is not the enemy you toil with,
> but rather a loved one reaching out a helping hand,

> to pull you from the drowning internal surroundings you find yourself in,

> *but words mean nothing in a fixated state of aphasia-*
> *muffled and worthlessly overlooked in a sea of misinformation.*

This is not the first time I have tried to redeem you,
> to grant you peace.

> *Even though it is not my job,*
> *nor my responsibility.*

And you are not the only one I have tried to save,
      and you probably will not be the last.

You are not broken,
      only misshapen-

      a result following from every experience,
      that has unfortunately inflicted its trajection along your path.

I love you,
      I pray for you,

      to release your burdening preconceptions-
      the bounded weight onto your feet.

      I pray for you to be set free.

2 Corinthians 4:17-18

For our light affliction,
which is for the moment,

works for us more and more
exceedingly an eternal weight of glory,

18 while we don't look
at the things which are seen,

but the things which are not seen.

For the things which are seen are temporal,

but the things which
are not seen are eternal.

A Eulogy for the Girl I Used to Be

There is something about the ending of chapters-
a close comparison to a current drawing out waters.

what once flooded my surroundings has gone away beyond my control.

The things it carries with its departures and what it leaves behind-
has all grown familiar to me.

So often the circumstances leaving me melancholy.

The loss of familiarity will haunt me and cloud the vision of my present reality-
finding myself eager for the fruition of futuristic fantasies to take life.

As the stories manifest off the pages from the storybook I write-
I hypocritically attempt to cling to the storyline I have long preside.

I like vacations-

a planned escape through a legal backdoor away from places of change,
favored over an irreversible permanent development.

It is embedded in my DNA-
a humanistic trait exemplified by my anxious thoughts of grey.

I mourned the loss of my girlfriend's parents as if they were my own,
without further understanding of the betterment the future would hold.

I gripped my pillow as I silently cried out the night of my last day of school-
as if I felt the last drops of sand fall from the expiring hourglass of my youth.

And I felt the air leave my chest when he precipitously dissipated from my view-
the re-entry of life-giving substance came with elongated resistance,

but not for him who held the key to my heart.
I am a permanent summer home when he needs to rest his head.

I never did quite breathe the same again-
living on life support of man-made oxygen.

My best friend takes notice as I hold every inhale I take in-
slow to exhale as I test the precious life I live.

The inevitable life and death cycles shaking me,
while watching the collapse of legacies around me.

The separation of a life-long unconditional love broke me.
I felt as though I poorly prioritized my time,

steering away from the path I thought God originally wrote for me-
with guilt reigning over me.

I have come to learn no experience nor amount of pain is without fertility.

It's taken great contemplation to insure stability,
    of the glass half-full mentality-

        nurturing the plans,
        the knowledge,
        the appreciation,

        the understanding of God's wants for me.

I can confidently say Calvinism's nihilism has not broken nor bound me.
    We do not experience in strife while the frontal lobe develops into maturity.

    I have hope.

These are the realizations I have had within my time here for a quarter century:
    1.Appreciate every day for what it is.

    2.Don't let the past water down the present.

    3.Kindness exhibits grace and respect.

    4.Spiritual fruit over material fruit.

    5.Sleep is essential.

    6.Being alone is okay.

    7.Do what you love.

    8.You are only as old as you feel.

    9.You can water the good or the bad- the choice is yours.

    10. God speaks when you're open to listen.

    11.Ephesians 6:12.

    12. Show kindness, but do not let others walk over you.

    13.Within life there is purpose.

    14.There is a spiritual gift within empathy.

    15.Appreciate community.

    16.Everyone has something they can teach you.

    17.The person you were, has transmuted you into the person you are.

    18.God is not always responsible, but He can always fix it.

    19.Listen more.

    20.Love is a simple yet catalyzing form of architecture.

    21.Baking without preheating results in your good works being underdone.

    22.God tests to bless, and the devil tempts to condemn.

    23.Quality over quantity.

    24.The fruits of the Spirit emerge from devotion.

    25.Change is not always comfortable, but it is okay.

                            This is what God has taught me. ♡

Notes

Page 9, Love is patient and is kind. Love doesn't envy. Love doesn't brag, is not proud,

5 doesn't behave itself inappropriately, doesn't seek its own way, is not provoked, takes no account of evil;

6 doesn't rejoice in unrighteousness, but rejoices with the truth;

7 bears all things, believes all things, hopes all things, and endures all things.
1 Corinthians 13:4-7, WEB.

Page 13, Yahweh is near to those who have a broken heart, and saves those who are crushed in spirit.
Psalm 34:18, WEB.

Page 17, Do not be deceived. God is not mocked, for whatever a man sows, that he will also reap.

8 For he who sows to his own flesh will from the flesh reap corruption. But he who sows to the Spirit will from the Spirit reap eternal life.

9 Let's not be weary in doing good, for we will reap in due season, if we don't give up.
Galatians 6:7-9, WEB.

Page 25, The woman said to the serpent, "We may eat fruit from the trees of the garden,

3 but not the fruit of the tree which is in the middle of the garden. God has said, 'You shall not eat of it. You shall not touch it, lest you die.'"

4 The serpent said to the woman, "You won't really die,

5 for God knows that in the day you eat it, your eyes will be opened, and you will be like God, knowing good and evil."
Genesis 3:2-5, WEB.

Page 27, For everything there is a season, and a time for every purpose under heaven.
Ecclesiastes 3:1, WEB.

Page 37, Don't remember the former things, and don't consider the things of old.

19 Behold, I will do a new thing. It springs out now. Don't you know it? I will even make a way in the wilderness, and rivers in the desert.
Isaiah 43:18-19, WEB.

Page 41, "For God speaks once, yes twice, though man pays no attention.

15 In a dream, in a vision of the night, when deep sleep falls on men, in slumbering on the bed."
Job 33:14-15, WEB.

Page 51, Don't be afraid, for I am with you. Don't be dismayed, for I am your God. I will strengthen you. Yes, I will help you. Yes, I will uphold you with the right hand of My righteousness.
Isaiah 41:10, WEB.

Page 65, He gives power to the weak. He increases the strength of him who has no might.
Isaiah 40:29, WEB.

Page 69, Blessed be the God and Father of our Lord Jesus Christ, the Father of mercies and God of all comfort;

4 who comforts us in all our affliction, that we may be able to comfort those who are in any affliction, through the comfort with which we ourselves are comforted by God.
2 Corinthians 1:3-4, WEB.

Page 77, In nothing be anxious, but in everything, by prayer and petition with thanksgiving, let your requests be made known to God.

7 And the peace of God, which surpasses all understanding, will guard your hearts and your thoughts in Christ Jesus.
Philippians 4:6-7, WEB.

Page 79, Don't boast about tomorrow; for you don't know what a day may bring.
Proverbs 27:1, WEB.

Page 87, "I have told you these things, that in me you may have peace. In the world you have trouble; but cheer up! I have overcome the world."
John 16:33, WEB.

Page 99, You count my wanderings. You put my tears into your container. Aren't they in your book?

9 Then my enemies shall turn back in the day that I call. I know this: that God is for me.

10 In God, I will praise his word. In Yahweh, I will praise his word.

11 I have put my trust in God. I will not be afraid. What can man do to me?
Psalm 56:8-11, WEB.

Page 103, I watch, and have become like a sparrow that is alone on the housetop.
Psalm 102:7, WEB.

Page 109, "Acquaint yourself with him, now, and be at peace. By it, good will come to you.

22 Please receive instruction from his mouth, and lay up his words in your heart.

23 If you return to the Almighty, you will be built up, if you put away unrighteousness far from your tents."
Job 22:21-23, WEB.

Page 121, Your word is a lamp to my feet, and a light for my path.
Psalm 119:105, WEB.

Page 123, Deliver me, Yahweh, from the evil man. Preserve me from the violent man:

2 those who devise mischief in their hearts. They continually gather themselves together for war.

3 They have sharpened their tongues like a serpent. Viper's poison is under their lips. Selah.

4 Yahweh, keep me from the hands of the wicked. Preserve me from the violent men who have determined to trip my feet.
Psalm 140:1-4, WEB.

Page 127, For our wrestling is not against flesh and blood, but against principalities, against the powers, against the world's rulers of the darkness of this age, and against the spiritual forces of wickedness in the heavenly places.

13 Therefore put on the whole armor of God, that you may be able to withstand in the evil day, and having done all, to stand.
Ephesians 6:12-13, WEB.

Page 133, And the Lord will deliver me from every evil work, and will preserve me
for his heavenly Kingdom. To him be the glory forever and ever. Amen.
2 Timothy 4:18, WEB.

Page 135, "Can a woman forget her nursing child, that she should not have compassion on the son of her womb? Yes, these may forget, yet I will not forget you!

16 Behold, I have engraved you on the palms of my hands. Your walls are continually before me."
Isaiah 49:15-16, WEB.

Page 141, Blessed is the man who doesn't walk in the counsel of the wicked, nor stand on the path of sinners, nor sit in the seat of scoffers;

2 but his delight is in Yahweh's law. On his law he mediates day and night.

3 He will be like a tree planted by the streams of water, that produces its fruit in its season, whose leaf also does not wither. Whatever he does shall prosper.
Psalm 1:1-3, WEB.

Page 145, Aren't five sparrows sold for assaria pennies? Not one of them is forgotten before God.

7 But the very hairs of your head are all counted. Therefore don't be afraid. You are of more value than many sparrows.
Luke 12:6-7, WEB.

Page 149, Therefore if anyone is in Christ, he is a new creation. The old things have passed away. Behold, all things have become new.
2 Corinthians 5:17, WEB.

Page 151, "Behold, I send you out as sheep among wolves. Therefore be wise as serpents and as harmless as doves."
Matthew 10:16, WEB.

Page 153, God said, "Let's make man in our image, after our likeness. Let them have dominion over the fish of the sea, and over the birds of the sky, and over all the livestock, and over all the earth, and over every creeping thing that creeps on the earth."
Genesis 1:26, WEB.

Page 159, "I am the true vine, and my Father is the farmer.

2 Every branch in me that doesn't bear fruit.

3 You are already pruned clean because of the word which I have spoken to you.

4 Remain in me, and I in you. As the branch can't bear fruit by itself unless it remains in the vine, so neither can you, unless you remain in me."
John 15:1-4, WEB.

Page 167, Not only this, but we rejoice in our sufferings, knowing that suffering produce perseverance,

4 and perseverance, proven character; and proven character, hope:

5 and hope doesn't disappoint us, because God's love has been poured into our hearts through the Holy Spirit who was given to us.
Romans 5:3-5, WEB.

Page 171, "I am the vine. You are the branches. He who remains in me, and I in him bears much fruit, for apart from Me you can do nothing.

6 If a man doesn't remain in me, he is thrown out as a branch and is withered; and they gather them, throw them into a fire, and they are burned.

7 If you remain in me, and my word remain in you, you will ask whatever you desire, and it will be done for you."
John 15:5-7, WEB.

Page 177, Oh, send out your light and your truth. Let them bring me to your holy hill, to your tents.

4 Then I will go to the altar of God, to God, my exceeding joy. I will praise you on the harp, God, my God.
Psalm 43:3-4, WEB.

Page 183, Behold, we call them blessed who endured. You have heard of the perseverance of Job, and have seen the Lord in the outcome, and how the Lord is full of compassion and mercy.
James 5:11, WEB.

For our light affliction, which is for the moment, works for us more and more exceedingly an eternal weight of glory,

Page 193, 18 while we don't look at the things which are seen, but the things which are not seen. For the things which are seen are temporal, but the things which are not seen are eternal.
2 Corinthians 4:17-18, WEB.

www.ingramcontent.com/pod-product-compliance
Lightning Source LLC
Chambersburg PA
CBHW051420090426
42737CB00014B/2752